HOW TO NEGOTIATE
YOUR SALARY

Tips, Gambits And Strategies
For Getting The Package You
Deserve

Alan Jones

D1413354

HOW TO NEGOTIATE YOUR SALARY

First published in paperback by Random Century Ltd 1992

Other books by Alan Jones: 'Winning At Interview' and 'Network To Get Work'

Cover design: www.creative-bytes.co.uk

Cover image: © Ficus24 1 Dreamstime.com

ISBN: 978-1479310845

CONTENTS

INTRODUCTION

CHAPTER 1 - *RESTORING THE BALANCE OF POWER*   *10*

An eye for the future - **CASE STUDY 1** - The price of failure - **CASE STUDY 2** - The negotiator as provider

CHAPTER 2 - *SO WHAT ARE YOU NEGOTIATING?*   *28*

What is 'TRP'? - What is negotiable? - **CASE STUDY 3** - Assembling the jigsaw - **CASE STUDY 4**

CHAPTER 3 - *SO WHAT ARE YOU SELLING?*   *46*

Identifying that 'Unique Selling Point' - **CASE STUDY 5** - What else can you bring to the party? - Eliminating the competition

CHAPTER 4 - *WHEN THE BARGAINING BEGINS*   *70*

Clarifying the objective - The dangers of compliance - Who are you talking to? - **CASE STUDY 6** - The role of the gatekeeper. - Pre-emptive and impulsive decision-making - **CASE STUDY 7** - Failure to reassure the gatekeeper

CHAPTER 5 - *ASSESSING THE BALANCE OF POWER*   *96*
Jockeying for position. - So, how important *is* money to you? - Pre-emptive and impulsive concession giving. - **CASE STUDY 8**. - To protect the vulnerable - **CASE STUDY 9** - Revealing the hidden objections - Selling your strengths and defending your weaknesses - Excess Baggage - Dress for success and strive to impress - The Go Between

CHAPTER 6 - *STRATEGY AND TACTICS OF NEGOTIATION*   *126*
Don't discuss the price until you've made the sale - So, what is your present salary?

- **CASE STUDY 10** - Body talk - An alternative response - What salary are you seeking (and are you worth it)? - **CASE STUDY 11** - Options for opening - **CASE STUDY 12** - That's where the money is - Job evaluation or person evaluation? - Considering the written offer - Considering your leverage and the 'nuclear option'

CHAPTER 7 - *NEGOTIATING FROM WITHIN* 178

Gently does it - Anticipating their objections - Preparing for the Appraisal - Considering the ultimatum

CONCLUSION

INTRODUCTION

Getting a job is only half of the battle - although you wouldn't know it from reading many books on job hunting. This book starts where others run out of ideas and grind to a halt. We will go where they fear to tread and discover how to get the best price for your labor.

Many of us accept jobs at a salary lower than we might have achieved - if only we had tried to negotiate a better deal. And as we'll see later some of us are denied offers through our *failure* to negotiate. But no one has ever lost a job worth having through tactfully asking for more money. The very idea of negotiating salary conjures up unedifying visions of eyeball-to-eyeball confrontation with complete strangers who have the power to award or withhold job offers, and who appear to hold all the aces. The ability to bargain is not highly developed in the average job hunter. But it need not be like that. If you feel that your negotiating skills could benefit from some fine-tuning then this book is for you.

But there's more to negotiating successfully than just developing the ability to do it. Ability must be preceded by *desire*. As 'employees' the desire to achieve a greater reward for what we do is not lacking - only the desire to make it happen. This is the great attraction of collective pay bargaining. How much more comfortable it is for us to have a third party doing our negotiating for us. The idea that there is something mildly indecent about discussing salary is well ingrained in our psyche but has no foundation in truth. After all, in 'Winning At Interview' we saw that the jobs market is a market place like any other and that the relationship between 'employer' and 'employee' is one of buyer and seller. As such there is a contractual obligation by one party to perform certain designated tasks in return for which the other party will pay an *agreed* sum of money and perhaps other benefits. Because the 'Why?' is as important as the 'How' this traditional reluctance to negotiate is explored in **Chapter 1.**

Negotiating a pay rise after already having secured a job is potentially more tough as other elements are brought into play - relationships have been developed which may or may not enhance your case, and attempting to move the goal-posts after the game has started may not endear you to some. In **Chapter 7** the differences between negotiating your salary and *re-negotiating* from within are discussed.

The act of negotiating salary need not be highly sophisticated. More often than not it's a rudimentary or even crude affair. Yet we must be mindful that the people, circumstances and situations that form the backdrop to such negotiations can be complex. For this reason the advice given here should not be seen as prescriptive. The over-riding aims are to explore the issues, de-mystify the process and to encourage you to maximize your earnings and ensure the buyer still gets *value for money*. It is then for you to interpret any advice in the light of your needs and circumstances.

Keep an open mind and resist the temptation to make assumptions. Move away from any stereotyped image of what you perceive the 'company' or the 'employer' to be. Any perceptions you hold will be borne out of your previous experiences but not everyone is out to get you as cheaply as possible. Nor are they all well-established, well-organized or equipped 'human resource' specialists well versed in the art of recruitment. It's well worth bearing in mind that we don't negotiate with employers - we negotiate with *people*, each one of whom has, at one time or another, sat on the opposite side of the negotiating table.

CHAPTER 1

RESTORING THE BALANCE OF POWER

Are all salaries negotiable - and if not why not?
Buyers who baulk at submitting themselves to
the joys of pay bargaining with sellers might
respond in one or all of the following ways:

- 'We can't have hundreds of people doing
the same work but all on different salary
scales. It would be an administrative
nightmare.'

- 'Parity on pay must be maintained for
those doing identical tasks - it would be
unfair and bad for morale to do
otherwise.'

- 'We know what the job is worth and
what we can afford to pay - we can
always get someone to do the job at the
price we set.'

The first response is no more than a volley of
verbal chaff devised to put potential salary
negotiators off the scent. With today's

technology the 'administrative nightmare' scenario no longer holds water.

The second response can be sustained for some types of organization such as the armed services but not in others. People may well carry out identical tasks but do they achieve the same results? Common sense dictates that performance related pay (where performance can be judged) is more likely to boost incentive and morale.

The third response is chilling in all its shoulder shrugging significance, for it strikes at the very nub of the power balance between buyer and seller - 'You need a job. We have a vacancy but don't necessarily need *you* to fill it. We are offering a fair salary so take it or leave it.' Not much room for negotiation there you might think.

As sellers in the 'jobs market' we presume too readily that the balance of power is weighted on the side of the buyer. Often this is the case but not always quite as much as you might think. It's all too easy to assume that there's no room for maneuver and that attempting to enter into a meaningful dialogue on the remuneration is at best a waste of time and at worst career suicide. A healthy mental response to the above statement would be along the lines of 'Once I've convinced you that you *do* need *me* to fill this vacancy we will negotiate.' The alternative is to tamely surrender and accept the offer as it stands.

The first lesson then is to assume that *all* salaries are negotiable. For sure, there's either room for negotiation or there's not but the only way to find out is to negotiate. In **Chapter 2** we'll consider the 'when?' and the 'how?' But for the moment we must proceed with the 'why?'

The very idea that we should politely request more money to be put on the table is anathema to many people when they are seeking work. But it's a cast iron certainty that many salaries that would have been negotiable never got negotiated. To understand why we need to look a bit more closely at the relationship between 'employer' and 'employee'.

Note: I gave the following advice at the beginning of 'Winning At Interview' and I make

no excuses for repeating it here for it underpins
everything:

Question to an employee: 'What is a job?'

Answer: 'It's a means of fulfilling my personal
needs in terms of income, professional
fulfillment, career progression and status.'

Question to an employer: 'What is a job?'

Answer: 'It's a means of profitably fulfilling the
needs of my organization.'

Clearly then for both parties a job is a means of
fulfilling needs - *but not the same needs.* To the
employer *their* needs are of over-riding
importance, and employing people is frequently
(although less frequently) the only way to fulfill
those needs. This is not to imply that employers
have complete disregard for those in their
employ, but during the recruitment process the
central question for them is *'what can you do for
us?'* Only when you have answered this
question might they begin to show a keener
interest in what they might do to fulfill *your*
needs.

As we'll see later, this can have a crucial bearing on the timing and conduct of the negotiation process. But just as importantly your understanding of this business relationship underpins your approach to selling yourself in the market place before and during interviews. This is a point well made by Richard Bolles in his excellent *'What Color Is Your Parachute?'* 'You're not visiting an employer in order for him or her to do *you* a big favor. If you've done your homework, you know you can be part of the solution there and not part of the problem.' Your attitude must not be one of 'job beggar.'

And yet the 'job beggar' position is exactly that adopted by most sellers. That's why they fail to sell themselves effectively and why they don't win offers for jobs that they should have won. And yes, that is why they destroy any base they might have had from which to negotiate salary with any degree of confidence and self respect.

Given then that the strength of your negotiating base is determined, in part, by your understanding of the need to sell and your ability to do so, the next question has to be 'So what are you selling?' In **Chapter 3** we'll be looking more closely at this but for now let's consider the potential dangers inherent in your adopting a weak and negative approach to the job search and salary negotiation:

An eye for the future

One of the more common results of the 'job beggar' attitude as outlined above is not simply that opportunities to negotiate a higher salary are missed but that, even more alarmingly, 'job beggars' are too inclined to accept offers at a *lower* salary than previously held. It must be said that taking a drop in salary is not a cardinal sin. For example, if your need in career terms is to change direction and move from a comparatively well paid profession such as banking to one less well paid such as social work then a drop in salary is almost inevitable. But if your need is to change jobs within the same profession then compromising on salary can have a very real downside:

CASE STUDY 1

Sarah had held positions of increasing responsibility, and remuneration, within the hi-tech industry. Her most recent job as a Systems Manager had become redundant, thus launching her into the jobs market. As a result of conducting an unprofessional job-search an interview was not forthcoming until three months down the track. At that interview the dialogue went something like this:

Buyer: What was your last salary?

Sarah: Sixty thousand a year

Buyer: (sharp intake of breath) - We can only offer fifty-five

Sarah: That won't be a problem - I guessed I'd have to take a salary drop.

Sarah was grateful enough to be offered the job but not happy with the salary drop - it had taken long hours and commitment to haul herself up to her previous paycheck. But on the other hand:

- It was her first offer and after three months on that emotional roller coaster of a job search she was eager to get off. Her financial resources were fast dwindling. Could she afford to turn it down? Had she just got lucky? When would the next offer come - another three months?

- It was otherwise a good job and they did promise a salary review in six months

- Her family and friends were encouraging her to take it. It was after all an income and she could still carry on job hunting

- She could *afford* to take a drop in salary

So Sarah took the job. Six months later that job became redundant; another job search, another interview:

Buyer: What was your last salary?

Sarah: Fifty five thousand

Buyer: We can only offer fifty but it will be reviewed in six months

There are many lessons we can learn from **Case Study 1** and they'll be addressed in later chapters but for now remember that:

- Poor job search = few interviews = fewer job offers = a weak negotiating base. A job offer, and in particular the first job offer, in isolation from other job offers gives you, unless you are good at playing hardball, a weak negotiating hand. If you have other offers you have *leverage*

- The promise of a salary review at some time in the future is a useful get out of jail card for the buyer, who may not be around in six months even if you are

- There's no doubt that it takes a certain chutzpah to turn down an offer in difficult circumstances; friends and relatives may apply pressure. But have no doubt; the idea that you'll carry on job hunting is perhaps the grandest act of self-delusion. Your new job, however 'lightweight' it may be, will require a learning curve that leaves no time, nor inclination, to job hunt. By the time you've come through that new relationships will have been formed, others will be depending upon you, you will have adjusted your life-style and inertia will take a grip. Apart from all of that you'll also figure (with some justification) that it might not be a great idea to change employers so quickly - 'it won't look too good on the résumé.'

- You must make a distinction between what you can afford to do and the wisdom of actually doing it. Just as buyers make a distinction between what they can afford to pay and what they are prepared to offer. *You are only as good as your last job and only as good as your last paycheck*

But for sure the biggest lesson of all is to conduct your affairs in such a way that your negotiating position is strengthened, not just this time around, but *for the next time* which, as Sarah found to her cost, came sooner than expected. It should be readily understood by now that there's no job security but it's surprising how many people, who have already had their fingers burned, expect their next job to last for as long as they need it to. It's not unusual to see those people going *down* the salary scale with each subsequent change of job.

This Case Study has painted a gloomy picture but necessarily so as this chapter is exploring the reasons we fail to negotiate salary. In **Chapter 6** we'll discover how the question ' What was your last salary?' might have been answered more effectively, but what was the fundamental reason for Sarah's reluctance to negotiate? *Fear*, based on the belief that:

- The balance of power was weighted totally on the side of the buyer. No cards to play

- Any attempt to negotiate would negate the offer

Have these fears any foundation in truth? To some extent yes. The balance of power was certainly in the hands of the buyer because:

- Sarah had, during the interview, let it be known that she'd been job-hunting for three months, unsuccessfully, having achieved no offers and with no interviews on the horizon

- She failed to identify what salary they were thinking of offering

- She disclosed her last salary, which drew a line in the sand and gave them a baseline from which to make an offer

With some forethought and pre-planning *all* of these hazards could have been avoided - thus restoring the balance of power and strengthening her hand. But, given that she held a weak hand, would any attempt at negotiating have ruined her chances of securing the offer? It would be most unlikely. This question will be more clearly answered in Chapters **5 and 6**, where we'll see how successful negotiation is determined not just by attitude but by timing, tactics, preparation and not least, the strength of the competition.

The price of failure

We saw in **Case Study 1** how failure to negotiate can secure an offer but at a lower salary than might have been achieved. But at least the offer was still on the table. Sarah's fear was that any attempt to negotiate would lose her the job. Perversely, there are circumstances where *failure* to engage in negotiations with the buyer can encourage them to withdraw any offer they were thinking of making.

To see how this can happen let's look at our next Case Study:

CASE STUDY 2

Michael was job-hunting from a position of strength. He had a job as Assistant to the Materials Manager with a firm of building contractors. He'd applied for the job of Materials Manager with another company. It would be a good career move. He already knew that the company advertising was offering a salary higher than his present one as they had 'opened at a price' in their advertisement. In most respects he was a good candidate for the job and the meeting with the CEO was progressing well. The conversation turned to the subject of finance:

CEO: How important is money to you?

Michael: Well, it's important but there are other things of equal importance such as job satisfaction and my personal career development. The salary isn't the 'be all and end all.'

CEO: How about a 70k base salary plus the usual benefits - is that acceptable?

Michael: Yes, that'll do just fine.

Other matters were discussed and the meeting ended amicably. Michael didn't get the offer. As the CEO explained to me ' He was a strong candidate for the job and I liked him. But throughout the meeting I'd deliberately stressed the point that we needed someone to get out there and negotiate the best prices for raw materials from our suppliers. His 'head to head' experience of this was limited and though he expressed his enthusiasm for it there was little hard evidence of his ability to do it well. I gave him the chance to negotiate a better price for his talents but he chose not to do it. If he can't negotiate his own package when invited to do so he'd be no good to me out there with these hard-nosed guys we have to deal with. Whether I would have improved my offer wasn't the point - if only he'd tried that might have given me the evidence I needed.'

What lessons can we learn from **Case Study 2**?

- At these meetings you are selling your skills. Negotiating is a skill and there are many jobs that, in one way or another, require such a skill. The buyer needs hard evidence from you that you have it. What better way to sell it than display it during the meeting?

- Even if you're negotiating from strength and know the salary is an improvement on your existing salary - negotiate!

- Don't assume that the subject of salary is being raised when it isn't. Any misinterpretation of the question 'How important is money to you?' can (as it did in this case) get you sucked into a premature discussion on the salary, which is *never in your best interests*. A different interpretation of, and response to, this question will be discussed in **Chapter 5**

- Be alert to any signals, verbal or visual, which indicate the salary is negotiable. In the above Case Study the question '...Is that acceptable?' implies that if it isn't then there's room for negotiation. It is an invitation to negotiate. Why turn down such an attractive invitation?

All things considered, **Case Study 2** is a classic example of snatching defeat from the jaws of victory. Even though the balance of power was, right from the outset, weighted more evenly than **Case Study 1** the seller failed to capitalize on it. In this example the failure was based not on fear but on *ignorance.*

Perhaps the greatest irony of all is that through the lack of feedback that bedevils all sellers, Michael would continue to make the same mistake at subsequent interviews and become paranoid about his 'interview technique.'

The negotiator as provider

Throughout this chapter we've seen how reluctance to negotiate is often based on fear and ignorance, and more often both. But does it go deeper than this? Quite possibly any distaste for negotiation might be based on the idea that it's an exercise in selfishness and greed.

At the time of writing Western economies in particular are in deep recession and the jobs market generally is depressed. Consequently there are more sellers than buyers. Under these circumstances having a job, almost at any price, is for many a success in itself, and to request more money for the privilege of working might seem to some as avaricious in the extreme.

The prevailing economic climate does have an important bearing on the balance of power between seller and buyer. When the economy is strong the demands upon the labor market are heavy and as a result companies competing with each other for a diminishing pool of human resources may have to offer incentives in the form of larger salaries. Although this economic seesaw is an important consideration when deciding how hard one should bargain it would be too simplistic to say that *no* salaries are negotiable in a recession. There are markets within markets and the global issue of supply and demand, although part of the equation, can too easily act as a smoke-screen when considering individual cases - a side-show to the main event which is that job seekers have a duty to *provide* not just, or even, for themselves but for their dependants. Any ambivalence towards negotiation should thus be tempered by this realization.

CHAPTER 2

SO WHAT ARE YOU NEGOTIATING?

What is 'TRP'?

The 'TRP' or 'Total Remuneration Package' is the sum total of benefits which accrue from a particular job, of which basic salary forms only a part. Many jobs *only* have a salary with no 'bells and whistles' or identifiable 'add-on's.' But when deciding on the *worth* of a job in financial terms you must take in to account the *value* of other benefits besides base salary. Failing to take this into account can have serious implications for the negotiation process:

- You could negotiate a higher salary than previously commanded but in real terms be worse off than before

- You could turn down an offer at a lower salary than previously commanded yet subsequently realize that you would have been better off in overall terms

- During the interview the TRP may be outlined but not with any great clarity.

Under the stress and strain of the interview your mental computations and comparisons with your existing/last job may be incorrect. Any misjudgment may diminish your enthusiasm and this will, visibly if not verbally, communicate itself to the buyer. The net result could be failure to even secure the offer, *leaving you with no decision to make*

The range of benefits can vary but they might typically include:

- Non - contributory pension
- Use of a car (business/private use)
- Private health scheme
- Subsidized travel
- Subsidized meals
- Stock options
- Bonus (guaranteed/performance related)
- Subsidized mortgage
- Discount on company goods/services

The computations can then be confusing in the white heat of a meeting. Your starting point before any meeting is to do your homework and have a clear understanding of where you are right now i.e. what your present/last job is/was worth to you in terms of TRP.

What is negotiable?

Much will depend on the flexibility of the employing company/organization. Some firms offer what is colloquially called the 'cafeteria' or 'menu' system of remuneration where they cost out the individual elements of the TRP to arrive at a total figure. Sellers are then invited to select their own 'menu' according to their needs. This system has caught on in some countries but not so much in others. However, even with this flexibility, it might still be a mistake for you to presume there's no leeway for negotiation on certain parts of the package. We can see just one example of how this can happen by looking at **Case Study 3**:

CASE STUDY 3

Mark achieved an interview during which the package was clearly outlined. It included base salary plus non-contributory pension, private health care and company car. He figured out easily that although the base salary was the same as in his last job, and he *had* been looking to improve on that, he'd still be better off because his last role had not included private health care, which he'd funded out of his own net income. Because the job had been advertised Mark knew he had competitors. He'd also discovered he was on a short-list of five. The company's need was urgent and they wanted someone to start soon. Mark had the advantage because he was out of work and could start straight away - his competitors had to serve one month's notice with their current employers. The balance of power was on Mark's side. He now had to decide whether to negotiate, when to negotiate and on what to negotiate.

Though the company wanted a quick decision Mark chose not to negotiate there and then but to keep his eyes on the prize and go all out to get the written offer. The dialogue went as follows:

Interviewer: Would you accept this job if we offered it to you?

Mark: On the basis of what we've discussed I'm really enthusiastic. How soon could you get a written offer to me and how soon after that would you need my decision?

Interviewer: Ok - I've one other person to see today and I can't pre-empt anything but you'll likely receive a written offer by Friday and we'll need to know by Monday.

Mark received the offer on Friday and had the weekend to consider his options. The offer was exactly as outlined at the meeting. He was clear in his mind that the job was right for him and that it would sit well on his résumé for the next time he was in the market, and that *they'd* made a good decision in offering it to him. He felt confident that he could negotiate a higher salary but instead decided to look more closely at his *needs*. The car on offer was adequate for business use but inadequate for leisure/family use so he successfully negotiated a larger vehicle. His increased costs for running a larger car were more than offset, as he no longer had to pay for private health care. The extra cost to the company was minimal and certainly less than if Mark had chosen to negotiate a higher salary.

Case Study 3 demonstrates that:

- The balance of power can also be influenced by factors other than attitude, i.e. the strength of the competition, urgency of the buyers' need and your ability to satisfy it. Even coming from a position of unemployment can be a selling point, as your competitors may have to give notice to their present employer

- You must be prepared to *justify* your reasons for negotiating. It's not unreasonable to assume that any attempt to negotiate a better deal will be met with the response ' why should we?' It's helpful for you to be able to answer this question with a justification that goes further than saying 'I'm worth it.' Inability to justify can weaken your negotiating position and meet with greater resistance

- Although Mark chose not to negotiate on more than one aspect of the 'TRP' you can try to negotiate on multiple aspects. Yet you must be realistic. Some top entertainers, sports stars etc can virtually name their price because of their uniqueness in the marketplace - the more rare the skills the greater the bargaining power. But for a job as Engineering Manager with a trucking company the scope may be limited. Distinguish then between *need* and *desire,* or if you prefer, *need* and *greed.* Buyers rarely get their sums so wrong that *all* aspects of the package are upwardly negotiable. Mark distinguished between his *desire* for a higher salary and his *need* for a larger vehicle. His decision was a sensible one

- The interview rarely provides the best platform from which to negotiate. Don't allow yourself to be 'steamrollered' into a negotiating position. Put all your energies into winning the prize and getting the offer. *Don't discuss the price until you've made the sale*

Your objective is to get from first base to written offer without negotiating or even discussing the salary / package and that takes a great deal of self-discipline which most sellers don't have. Why? Because they are so burning up with curiosity to find out what the salary is that they give the buyer all sorts of opportunities to raise it. We'll see later that it isn't always possible to delay the salary discussion and you won't always be able to do anything about it. But to give a common example let's look again at the last Case Study. Imagine you've just about jumped through all the hoops and got yourself to the final interview but they've given no indication of what package they are thinking of offering:

Interviewer: Would you accept this job if we offered it to you?

Now this is a common question at the end of a final meeting. It's a very strong 'buy' signal and so a great question to get. But if the price hasn't been discussed you'd be sitting there thinking 'How can I answer that - I don't know what you're going to pay me?' Now if you were not careful that would impel you to do what everyone else does. You'd snatch defeat from the jaws of victory and respond by saying either 'Yes, depending on terms and conditions' or the more coy 'Yes, but we haven't discussed everything yet' or the crass and pompous 'I can't make a decision until I have something in writing' (**What's your problem - don't you trust me?**). You may even threaten the buyer 'I'm enthusiastic but I do have other things to consider.' Never threaten the buyer with the leverage that you may have other offers because human nature kicks in big time (**Well you just go away and consider them then - you've blown it**) That you may have other offers should be the sword of Damocles that you have subtly placed over their head. But once you start waving it around you lose.

Far better to infer from the question that they *are* offering it to you and close it down by responding as Mark did: 'On the basis of what we've discussed' is a caveat 'I'm really enthusiastic' which is as close to 'yes' as you should go. Now ask 'How soon could you get a written offer to me?' because that's a non-crass way of saying 'I can't answer that until I have it in writing'. And finally ' and how soon after that do you need my response?' Now that's a non-threatening way of saying ' think carefully about your price because I'm not going to bite your hand off. I've got other things to consider and want to know how much time I've got to pull it all together.'

Now they're either offering it to you or they're not. If they're not they would back-peddle and say ' **Whoa - we haven't reached that point yet - I'm just trying to find out if you're interested in the job**.' All you have to do now is re-state your interest.

If they *are* offering it to you then you get ' **Well, we can get a written offer to you by Friday and we'd need your response by next Monday.**' At which point you should already be standing up, reaching for your hat and coat, and shaking their hand 'You've made my day' and getting the hell out of there. Don't stick around and carry on selling - you've got an offer on the way.

Assembling the jig-saw

We saw in Chapter 1 how the balance of power can be equalized by overcoming fear and ignorance. We also saw how that balance of power can be influenced by other factors such as the strength of the competition, the urgency of the buyer's need and your ability to satisfy that need. Given that knowledge = strength = power what additional knowledge is it in your interests to gain - which in turn will give you the confidence to negotiate? A job interview is no different from a sales meeting and such meetings are not unlike a jigsaw puzzle. Prior to the meeting you need to have assembled as many of the pieces as possible. It is surprising that many job applicants are given the chance to assemble the pieces yet choose not to do so. Consider the following invitation to an interview:

' Dear Mr. Black,

 Further to your application for the above position we are pleased to invite you for an interview at 2pm on Wednesday 25 October. When you arrive at the above address please ask to see Mrs. Hilary Brown.

Yours sincerely,

Victor Newman

HR Manager '

Not all invitations to interview are as curt as this but many are. Which pieces of the jigsaw are they providing?

1. Location of meeting

2. Date of meeting

3. Time of meeting

What pieces are missing?

1. Name and job title of interviewer(s)

2. Objective of meeting

3. Likely duration of meeting

Time and again, three of the most vital pieces of information crucial to the success of any sales meeting are exactly those that are omitted. Not deliberately of course. But no professional sales person would consider turning up to such a meeting without previously establishing exactly *who* will be in attendance, *how long* it is likely to last and *what the objective* is. Unfortunately, when we are seeking a job this is exactly what we do.

As a potential negotiator you don't want any surprises. Your words and action will, to a large extent, be influenced by your knowledge of the audience. The above invitation is ambiguous - who is Mrs. Hilary Brown? She could be anyone in the organization from the receptionist to the CEO. You may assume that she is the person who will be interviewing you. You may look her up on their web site. You may do a LinkedIn/Google search etc on her. Yet stories are legion of sellers not clarifying who they will be seeing, turning up on the day and being led by a 'Mrs. Brown' like a lamb to the slaughter into an imposing board-room to be confronted by a panel of six strangers. Now *that's* a surprise you don't need. You might also assume that the author of the invitation will be in on the meeting but *assume nothing*.

Expecting the buyer to state the objective of the meeting in their invitation might, you think, be asking them to state the obvious: the overall aim of the meeting is for them to assess if you can do the job and for you to assess the same and decide if you want to do it - isn't it? Wrong! What you really want to know here is the *game plan*. Is this a 'one-off' meeting or a preliminary meeting with a 'short-list' meeting at some subsequent and as yet undefined point in the future? If it's the first of a series of meetings then your primary objective is to make it through to the next one - not jump in feet first with some outrageous financial demand.

You have a right to know, and a need to know, the anticipated duration of the meeting. You're busy and have other commitments. If you don't then there's something seriously wrong with your job search campaign. But the importance of your establishing the time factor goes much deeper than simply your desire to arrange your other affairs. The over-riding reason is best illustrated by **Case Study 4:**

CASE STUDY 4

Marc was invited to an interview but not briefed on timing or the structure of the process. Quite rightly he telephoned to confirm attendance and established that this was a first meeting with the HR manager, at the end of which a short-list would be drawn up and the successful candidates would be met, two weeks later by, as yet, a person or persons unknown. Unfortunately, Marc omitted to establish just how long the first meeting was expected to last.

On meeting the HR manager the usual preliminary 'small talk' revealed there was a common link between them in that they had both, in the distant past, been members of the same club. The next twenty minutes were devoted to an enjoyable discussion about the club. Both parties were taking a trip down memory lane. Marc was happy to go along with this. There was, after all, plenty of time - wasn't there?

Unfortunately there wasn't time at all. The HR manager made heroic efforts to recover the situation but had left only ten minutes to explain the nature of the role, ask Marc pertinent questions about his relevant experience and assemble the evidence upon which to base a recommendation that he be seen again. That meeting over-ran by ten minutes - so, an interview only scheduled for 30 minutes had taken 40, and fifty per cent of that time was spent, not on the objective, but on irrelevant chat. As Marc said 'I wasn't surprised not to get the second interview - I felt when I came away from the meeting that I hadn't sold anything at all. I wasn't given the opportunity but then I assumed we had plenty of time.'

Assume nothing! There's nothing unique about the above Case Study. In its various guises it shows up time and time again. Never assume that interviewers know how to conduct interviews, nor even that they enjoy interviewing or want to interview you. If you discover before turning up that you have just 30 minutes then as soon as you meet the buyer, at the earliest opportunity (if you let the hares start running and they are wasting time it's too late to do anything about it) say to the buyer 'Am I right we've about half an hour?' That's often all it takes to make them get down to business. Alternatively, if you establish that they have allocated more time then you don't need to panic if they talk irrelevances for a while.

These meetings do have a habit of under and over running but you are at a real disadvantage if you turn up not knowing where the end is at least meant to be.

If you're going to a meeting to sell something then you must know how much time you've got to make the sale. Apart from anything else it will dictate your *pace*.

If you don't do your homework and remove uncertainty by assembling the jigsaw then you may not even get to the negotiating table.

A word of caution; telephone calls can work against you as well as for you. The potential 'dangerousness' of the call lies in its unpredictability. You can never be sure who's going to pick up the phone. It could be the person you'll be meeting and you could end up being interviewed over the phone, which will not be in your best interests if you're unprepared. Besides securing vital information your objective is to 'make a friend at court' and score a few points by displaying the initiative to take certain businesslike actions that at this early stage set you apart from your competitors. But be sensitive to what is going on at the other end. If they are busy they won't want a stranger asking a long string of questions.

CHAPTER 3

SO WHAT ARE YOU SELLING?

A fundamental rule of salary negotiation is that sellers should always avoid a buyer's market. In a buyer's market the balance of power is not on the side of the seller. But fundamental rules are one thing - reality can be quite another. The reality for most job seekers is that through redundancy or other pressing personal needs they have no choice in the matter. But take heart, selling in a buyer's market doesn't in itself mean that you've no cards to play. It does means you will have to work harder to sell. The more effectively you sell the stronger your ultimate negotiating position. Obviously, we're not all selling identical things and even during the same job search you may be selling different things to different employers.

Let's hope that your competitors turn up for the meeting with the objective of getting a job. You're turning up to demonstrate that you can solve their problem by contributing good things.

Time then, to draw up a menu of your own. In general terms, what combination of 'good things' can you contribute that the organization might just want to buy? (Whether it actually *does* want to buy them we shall deal with later.)

- Experience
- Skills
- Achievements
- Qualifications
- Personality
- Commitment
- Initiative

These are just a few to be going on with. They bear closer inspection:

Experience

This is in itself much over-rated, not least because it is, mistakenly, sold through *time*. '20 years experience in the media' only tells the buyer how long you've been at it. It isn't in itself an indicator of *how good* you are at it. Competitors with half that experience could be more 'on the ball', and what if they can sell themselves better than you? Many potential negotiators see their lack of experience as a real Achilles Heel and unwisely allow this to undermine their confidence - which in turn fosters a reluctance to negotiate. If you can effectively sell the experience you have then don't be concerned about the experience you lack. If you think the buyer has doubts about the quality of your *relevant* experience this 'hidden fear' can be accurately expressed as 'Because you haven't done this type of work before I doubt your ability to do it.' Now either you have enough relevant experience to solve the problem or you don't. If you do have that experience then sell it. But if you *don't* have it then you mustn't leave the meeting without having convinced them about your *ability to do it.*

This 'objection to the sale' is covered in more depth in 'Winning At Interview' but for now you can reassure the buyer on this by selling your confidence, enthusiasm, flexibility and your short learning curve. The importance of this 'reassurance factor' will become more apparent in later Chapters. When you win the prize and are subsequently offered the job your skill in having defended the 'lack of experience' objection can give you more negotiating leverage and/or have a bearing on whether you start on the lower, middle or upper end of a pay scale.

Skills

Selling your skills is an essential precursor to any dialogue on salary negotiation. You should not move, or be allowed to move, into any negotiating position until you have sold the skills, which, in your view, will enable you to do the job effectively. Sellers are often given to talking in vague terms about their 'experience' but have little or no understanding of what skills these experiences have given them. The assumption seems to be that it is the role of the buyer to deduce this information from astute questioning. But your role is to not to make their job any harder than it already is - quite the reverse. Those 2 out of 10 trained, experienced and *skilful* interviewers (yes 8 out of 10 people you're going to meet are untrained and inexperienced) will know how to extract this information - but even they will admit that it's often like extracting teeth. Help them all out by having clarity and doing your skills analysis.

Achievements

You are selling *success* and *the ability to get results*. This is why we pay people and this is why we might be willing to pay more to some people than to others. An obvious, though not foolproof, way for the buyer to figure out if you can get results is to drill down on your past achievements - your 'track record' provides the buyer with a body of evidence upon which to make an objective judgment. So, what have your previous experiences allowed you to achieve?

Admittedly, we're not much given to owning up to our achievements, and least of all boasting about them at interviews. But one thing is certain; there are always a lot of very able yet humble people in the jobs market, and a lot more working for a pittance. An excess of humility doesn't make for a strong negotiating position.

Be selective in selling your achievements. Now *your* greatest achievement may have been winning the North West Tango Dancing championships in 2007. But this might elicit not a few yawns if you're going to apply for a role as Area Manager of XYZ Steel Bearings Company. Be prepared to sell some lesser achievements if they are more relevant to the needs of the company.

It's not always possible to quantify achievements but don't hesitate to do so. Remember too that you are selling your *integrity* so don't divulge information they might consider confidential to your previous employer. Achievements that make buyers sit up and take notice are those that indicate your ability to save on costs and/or increase profits. The significance of this when it comes to negotiating salary will not be lost on you. Employers will be less reluctant to improve upon the level of remuneration if you can convince them they would be getting *value for money*.

Qualifications

Be careful, as this can be tricky. The issue of qualifications should not loom as large at the interview as it might at the application stage. The problem here could be in you having too many qualifications rather than too few. Over-selling is as dangerous as under-selling. It's really a matter of 'horses for courses.' You may have a Doctorate and you may have some justification in demanding a higher salary for it. But do they need it? And if not why should they incur an additional expense for something they don't need? Over-selling on the qualifications could encourage them to see you as 'too heavyweight' for the role. Only play this particular card when you have clarity on the extent of their needs.

Personality

This is not something you can easily put a price on but arguably you're selling this more than anything else at the meeting. Your personality and character is that combination of behavioral and psychological characteristics that identify you as being unique. They are sometimes described as the 'softer skills' or 'emotional intelligence'. A good salesperson must have plenty of personality. The type of personality they wish to buy may change depending on the role but in general terms, and certainly at executive level, they like to see a combination of:

- Confidence
- Positive mental attitude
- Self-esteem
- Enthusiasm
- Sense of humor
- Common sense
- Empathy

This is a happy co-incidence as these are exactly the qualities required by a good negotiator. The great irony is that when you're thrown unceremoniously into that viper's nest of a jobs market a lot of the above qualities take a severe testing and battering which can lead you into the 'job beggar' mind-set. This paradox can't be resolved by the flick of a switch but people are unlikely to buy something from those who appear to have no confidence in what they are selling - let alone be amenable to having the price increased. All potential buyers will also need to know 'Are you going to fit in?' You're in a much stronger negotiating position once you've convinced them that you're the kind of personality and character they want to have on board.

Commitment

You must of course display a degree of commitment to working for the organization but the issue here is often perceived *lack of commitment* to your profession. This can arise for those who, for a period of time, leave their profession in order to do something markedly different - a typical example being self-employment.

If you've left a previous job to set up on your own and the business failed, then your position will be such that a job search will provide the only realistic escape route. It does take a lot of admirable qualities to start up a business, certainly those listed above, but success takes, amongst other things, planning, vision and sound organizational skills. If your business failed then potential employers may question, however unfairly, those skills. You should be selling success, not failure, even though failure can teach positive lessons.

In addition, your motives for moving from employment to self-employment and back again may come under the microscope. If your original reasons for leaving your profession / vocation were negative then employers will be entitled to ask what has changed your feelings - apart from the fact that you are now in a bit of a hole.

Now this is not to suggest that you would never work again - that would be ludicrous. It is to say that if you interrupted a career that was professional / vocational then your commitment to that career may be questioned. You may gain re-entrance, but they may be reluctant to start you on a salary that does not exact some kind of price for your 'indiscretion'.

Initiative

This is a quality much in demand but scarce in supply. Yet how do you sell it? All very well at the meeting to say that you have it but you need the evidence, in the form of examples, to prove it. The best way to sell initiative is to *display it*.

Case Study 4 showed how 'piecing the jigsaw together' before the meeting can give you more confidence to negotiate salary. But quite apart from that considerable benefit, in carrying out the actions recommended you are displaying a great deal of initiative. A practical demonstration of what you are selling always impresses more - don't tell them if you can show them.

Identifying that unique selling point

Having identified that combination of 'good things' that you can bring to the organization your next step is to clarify in your own mind how many of them will most likely make the buyer really sit up. In other words what are your unique selling points? 'Unique' doesn't necessarily mean unique in the market place but unique in comparison to your competitors. In a tough market you must look for something that might give you the edge on the competition, just as any business would.

If the buyer has been assiduous during the earlier selection process then it's most likely that those who make it to the short list could all *do* the job. Your task now is to somehow convince them to offer it to you and not one of the others. You can go quite some way towards this by expressing your *desire* for it. This might seem self-evident but so many potential negotiators never got to negotiate because they omitted to say that they wanted the job! In a buyer's market they have an embarrassment of riches and it's a tough call deciding whom, from three top class candidates, to offer it to. All else being equal they may be more inclined to offer it to the one who *said* they wanted it.

Yet this in itself may not be enough. The buyer may still say 'Why should I choose this person? What can this person bring to my company that the others can't? It is your job to tell them and don't wait to be asked because they may not pose the question, neither to you nor themselves. If you don't sell your 'uniqueness' then chances are they'll toss a coin to get a result.

It may help to remember that employers may want you not just for the range of skills and talents you can bring to the role today but what you can do for them in the future. You may have a skill, knowledge or some talent not relevant to the job being discussed but relevant to them on a broader front. **Case Study 5** demonstrates this:

CASE STUDY 5

Carly was a marketing specialist with a background in the service industries, advertising, promotions, exhibitions etc. Her career had been spent mostly in the US and she was being interviewed for a senior marketing role based in New York. The company was young and ambitious and through her research, which included talking to her network contacts, she knew that the company was expanding into Europe, initially France. Carly's family were

French on her Mother's side and she could speak fluent French. None of this was of direct relevance to the role under discussion so the buyers at the final interview didn't raise it as a topic, and Carly chose not to raise it, as she was confident she would get the offer. The financial package was outlined but not negotiated at this stage.

On receipt of the offer Carly decided to accept but felt she had nothing to lose by asking the key question 'How negotiable is the package?' They made some reluctant noises about not wanting to set a precedent. Carly then played her ace by sending a follow up e-mail explaining that she could speak fluent French, had contacts in Paris and would be able to help them build a presence there. They re-shaped the role to accommodate this and greatly improved their offer.

There's much to learn from Carly's experience:

- **You may not identify your unique selling point until well into the recruitment process**. In the 'visible' market' i.e. advertised jobs, that process drags on for weeks if not months. The job is often re-shaped by the company during this period, sometimes so much that the job eventually offered bears little resemblance to that originally advertised, and because the traditionally slow recruitment process can't keep up with the pace of change going on out there right now the vacancy can disappear altogether - leaving you hugging an empty sack if you haven't kept your foot on the gas

- **Some buyers don't realize they need something until you start selling it to them**. That she could speak fluent French was on Carly's résumé but they didn't pick up on it as they saw it as irrelevant for the role in New York

- **Even if you identify a unique selling point you may choose to 'keep your powder dry' and not reveal it to the buyer until the optimum time for you**. Because Carly was confident of getting the offer she saw it as a bargaining chip to be used *after* the offer had been made. If she were not that confident then she would have been wise to have put it on the table as a selling point to clinch the offer, which would probably have diminished its value as a bargaining chip later on

- **Choose the right medium to negotiate**. You may feel that a face-to-face meeting would be best but it doesn't have to be a meeting they've called. As it's a two-way process sellers can call meetings so don't hesitate to say you'd like to meet them again to discuss a few things. Carly chose initially to make a call. Note how to frame the question. Never ask a closed question by saying 'Is the package negotiable?' because this invites the answer 'No it isn't'. As an open question 'How negotiable is it?' it implies that of course it's negotiable so how much extra can you find? But when playing the bargaining chip she chose e-mail as the medium. This gives the other party time, and it may be in your interests to give them that time, to consider their response. They may have to confer with others

- **'We can't set a precedent by giving you more than anyone else doing the same type of work'.** This is one of the toughest 'objections' to overcome. It again highlights the importance of being able to *justify* your position and maybe put something else on the table

What else can you bring to the party?

You may have some reservations about accurately identifying a skill or combination of skills which might be perceived as being unique - in which case you must look for something else. What you're seeking is some asset, which might encourage the buyer to offer the job to you as opposed to one of your competitors.

You're well set to identify such an asset if you're clear in your own mind about the company's needs. An advertisement for example is a problem crying out for a solution and little more than a 'shopping list' of the buyer's needs, some of which are more important than others. And if the advertisement has been well thought through it's easy for you to arrange their list in priority order. Look out for the tell-tale signs: the use of words and phrases like 'ideally' 'preferably' 'would be an advantage' 'likely' 'probably' all indicate they would settle for less if they had to. But those phrases are more common in a sellers market. In a buyers market you're more likely to read 'essential', 'must have' and 'will be' as they can be more choosey. But if you get the interview then yes, you can win the offer, though the more you make them compromise on their needs the weaker your eventual negotiating position. To counter this effectively you must be able to say 'I can't give you that but I can give you this or, if you can satisfy all their needs, 'I can not only give you all that but I can also give you this.'

We've already seen in **Case Study 5** that you need to think carefully about when and how to float the idea, but putting an extra asset on the table can make you more desirable. In some cases providing a useful extra talent over and above their needs can even obviate the requirement for them to recruit an additional person - freeing up extra cash, some of which might find its way to you.

So look carefully at what they need and why they need it. Then take a step back and ask yourself 'what other talent/asset can I bring which will make me even more desirable? This will naturally depend on the type of job, the nature of the business and your previous experiences. To get you thinking along the right lines here's some examples of the types of asset prized by many buyers:

- Marketing, training and financial experience

- Business contacts

- Inside knowledge of competing companies

- Recruitment, coaching, mentoring experience

- Language skills

- Knowledge or practical experience of health & safety, security etc

If you have an extra asset don't give it away but *sell it*. If you're unused to being in a bargaining or negotiating arena then the temptation for you to give it away will be immensely strong. This temptation for you to become the 'impulsive conceder' will no doubt derive from any feeling of vulnerability and failure to overcome the fear barrier. Remember that *low self-esteem courts failure* while a positive mental attitude and self-assurance engenders respect. In **Case Study 5** Carly was not a 'job beggar'. She was not saying to the company 'If you give me this job I'll give you my contacts and language skills for free.' Her message was ' I can satisfy all your stated needs but I also have more which you will find useful - if you agree let's put a price on it.' There is a world of difference between those two stances. In purely fiscal terms there was also a few thousand dollars worth of difference. Remember then that a high rarity value strengthens your negotiating position.

Eliminating the competition

Because the employer is the buyer it should be self evident that the onus is on the seller to take the dominant role. Yet traditionally this has not been the case in this particular market. As job hunters we've come to expect the employer to make the running, and this has encouraged a passive/reactive approach to the job search, which results in the employer appearing to hold all the aces. It's a peculiarity of the jobs market that it's the only market place where the buyer is *expected* to advertise a need. But you can reap huge benefits by adopting the traditional role of seller and taking what you're selling to the market place.

A job advertisement is a cry for help. It's a problem urgently seeking a solution and, in responding, sellers put themselves forward as the solution. They 'throw their hats into the ring', saying to the buyer 'see me - I can solve your problem'. Unfortunately there are perhaps 99 other hats being thrown into the same ring at the same time. They all convey the same message - 'see me, see me, me! me! me!' The buyer is spoilt for choice, will throw out most of the hats immediately, will try some on, remain undecided and end up hiring, maybe not the best person for the job (they were eliminated because they had lousy résumés) but the one who sold themselves the best. This all leaves far too much to chance and lengthens the odds on you even reaching the negotiating table. How then to reduce the odds?

Eliminate the competition! By ensuring you are the only seller you increase your chances not only of reaching the table but also of strengthening your negotiating position. You are removing from the buyer the element of choice (apart from 'take it or leave it'). This is not to suggest that the eventual salary will be any more negotiable - but it increases the possibility of it being so.

The 'window of opportunity', which allows you ultimately to negotiate from strength, is that period of time between when the need arises but before the buyer gets around to doing something about it i.e. advertising or briefing a recruitment firm.

Advertisements don't suddenly appear overnight. They are preceded by weeks if not months of pestering by line managers clamoring for more staff, meetings and discussions between department heads and HR, vacillation by directors - indecision upon indecision! You don't have a crystal ball but with careful research and your all-important networking it's sometimes possible for you to identify the need even before the buyer does. A well-timed direct/speculative approach may even lead to a job being created for you. The benefits of making the first approach must not be underestimated. They are:

- You are, at least potentially, eliminating the competition, which is perhaps the single most important factor influencing your negotiating power

- You are displaying initiative - as we've seen, a key selling point

- You are potentially saving the buyer time and money. Recruiting through the more conventional means costs big bucks in say, agency fees plus the hidden costs of tying up internal staff

When the window is open few things are set in stone. Once an ad is written, or an agency briefed, then the window is closing fast. 'Qualifications, 'experience' and 'competencies' can become fixed and they may be reluctant to go back on these. They're now looking for someone to 'shoe horn' into the role. It's in your interests to sell before they firm up on these things. When the window is open they are more amenable to making the role fit you and of course, you're maybe reaching them before they have made any pricing decision.

---------◆ ◆ ◆ ---------

CHAPTER 4

WHEN THE BARGAINING BEGINS

Clarifying the objective

So when does the bargaining begin? It depends.
As the seller you can't predict with certainty
when the buyer will decide to raise the subject
of price. One thing is for sure; you don't want it
to begin before it needs to begin. If you've
assembled the jigsaw correctly (Chapter 2) you'll
know whom you are seeing, for how long and
clarified the objective for the meeting. This
knowledge will give you the confidence to
achieve your objective and not get drawn into
any pre-emptive discussion on the salary issue.
It's certainly not for you to make a pre-emptive
strike and open up negotiations before the
buyers have decided that they want you. *Don't
discuss the price until you've made the sale.*

Neither should you confuse salary negotiation
with the initial 'jousting', which often takes
place at an early stage of proceedings.
Compliant sellers are knocked off their perch

early on by questions such as 'What's your present/last salary?' and 'What salary are you seeking?' Now this brings us to the tricky matter of 'opening at a price'. The rule is that whoever opens at a price is potentially, and only potentially, in the weaker bargaining position so try not to let it be you. In the visible jobs market, for example in job advertisements, the buyer will sometimes open at a price by stating the salary/package, but most often they will not. They will be coy and use weasel words like 'competitive' 'highly competitive' (I guess that's better than a 'competitive' salary?) or 'attractive' (now this is confusing - would you rather have an attractive salary or a competitive one?) - or how about 'negotiable'? You might prefer that but it often turns out to be no more negotiable than an attractive salary or any other salary. There is also, for very senior roles, the enigmatic yet enticing 'the remuneration will reflect the importance we attach to this position.' That'll get you salivating.

Now we mustn't allow paranoia to set in here. An advertisement is a public thing so anyone can see it. The information could be price sensitive and damaging if released to the outside world. For example, they might not want their competitors to know what they are paying their staff. They might not want other people in the company to know what they are paying for this role and, unfortunately, they might not want the current job - holder to know that they are going to pay his/her successor more money. Or of course they may have no idea what they should be paying because they may be as inexperienced at recruiting as you are at job hunting.

They will sometimes however demand to know your current or previous salary at the application stage. Employers are, thankfully, asking this less frequently as they've at last got around to the idea that this question is impertinent. The other request 'Give details of your salary expectations' is not at all impertinent as the buyer has a right to know what price you put on your services - as in any other market place. And yet you are still being asked to 'open at a price.' What do you do about it? Well, this might be the time to phone them and ask outright what they mean by 'attractive' etc because you don't want to waste their time. At this stage you haven't formally thrown your hat into the ring and you're anonymous. They are often more amenable about divulging the package over the phone. You may then decide not to apply at all or if you do apply you can figure out how it might weaken or strengthen your hand by divulging your price.

If a recruitment firm is involved the inherent downside for you is that they need a price to go on and digging your heels in can be counter productive. On the basis that you don't want to win the battle but lose the war you may prefer to open at your *aspirational price*. As a general rule if you're going to open then the package you are seeking is the one to go for as it gives you more options. If for example you are changing your career and seeking to move from a highly paid job into a sector where the pay is low then divulging your last salary might have them reaching for the smelling salts. So it might be safer to say 'my previous salary is irrelevant - better to talk about what I'm looking for I think'.

Incidentally, and here's an irony - it isn't always easy to persuade a buyer to pay you *less* than you were earning previously. You can protest as much as you like and they may smile and nod sagely but will most likely take the view that you won't really be happy with a drop in your standard of living and after a few months you'll leave in search of the big bucks.

The dangers of compliance

Divulging your present or previous salary/package is not a cardinal sin and you won't always be able to avoid it. For example, job hunting and recruitment is becoming more technology driven by the day and with some of these on-line applications if you don't fill in that box then it won't go anywhere. So you win some and you lose some. But it's worth being aware of the potential dangers of compliance with their request:

- **They will see that your present/most recent package is more than they are**

willing to pay, will assume that you won't be willing or able to drop to their price and put you on the rejection pile. Now you may have been willing to drop but won't get to first base to discuss it. And they sure won't phone you to ask if you'd be willing to drop. Why? Because they've got 199 other job applications sitting in front of them, and they are weeding out, not selecting in. It's important to understand that the initial selection process, which may only take 30 seconds, is really a *rejection* process. In that first pass they're most likely looking for those they are *not* going to meet

As a brief diversion, and just in case you still think this rejection/selection process is a sophisticated affair, a client of mine told me of the time he and his boss were recruiting and they were swamped by scores of résumés. He said to his boss 'How are we going to get through this lot - it'll take days?' 'No it won't' said his boss who randomly picked up most of the résumés and threw them in the garbage can.

My client was shocked and said 'Wha.... you can't do that - it's not fair'. His boss replied 'Yes it is, we don't want to hire anyone who's unlucky do we?'

- **The buyer will see that your present/most recent package is worth a good deal less than they are willing and able to pay.** In which case they may conclude that you're not 'heavy-weight' enough for the job and reject you. Or you may get the meeting and even get the offer further down the track but they'd be less likely now to pay you top dollar if they knew you had been earning less

Now none of this is to suggest that the buyer is making the wrong judgment calls here. They may be right that you won't stick around on a lower salary. They may be right that you're not 'heavy-weight' enough for the job. But that's not the point. The point is that you want to get to the meeting to discuss it.

Who are you talking to?

You've clarified whom you'll be meeting. But have you identified what *power* they have? Do they have the power to say 'yes - you're hired' or do they have the power to say 'You will go no further'? Do they have authority to negotiate salary? What is their relationship to others in the organization, and to whom you may be talking at a later stage? This 'backdrop' against which discussions and negotiations take place can determine your strategy, tactics and have a real bearing on the eventual outcome.

CASE STUDY 6

David had applied for the job as Assistant to the Chief Buyer for a medium sized firm in the food/beverage retail business. The 'backdrop' was not complicated. Just an initial interview with the Chief Buyer who would then draw up a short-list and arrange a final interview with himself and the CEO. They had given no indication of the package and David had given no information on existing package or expectations. At the first meeting with the Chief Buyer the conversation went like this:

Chief Buyer - What base salary are you asking for?

David - I guess 65 thousand.

Chief Buyer - We can do better than that!

David - What are you thinking of?

Chief Buyer Well I know the CEO is expecting to pay 70 but we can sort that out at the next stage.

At the next and final meeting with both the Chief Buyer and the CEO present the conversation went like this:

CEO - Tell me what salary you want.

David - I guess 70 thousand.

CEO - You're sure that would be acceptable to you?

David - Sure

David was offered and accepted the job at the indicated salary. When discussing this with the Chief Buyer some time later David asked him why he'd been so helpful with his advice on the salary. The Chief Buyer told David it was in his interests to get David's salary as close as possible to his. In a few months' time the Chief Buyer was going to re-negotiate his remuneration with the CEO and he wanted the leverage to say that his assistant was earning nearly as much as he was. He also knew that if David had opened at 65 thousand then the CEO might just agree to that.

The lessons to learn from **Case Study 6** are:

- You'll not *always* have to negotiate for them to increase the price - but don't put money on it

- The dynamic/relationship between you and the buyers(s) and that between the buyers themselves can have a crucial bearing on the outcome

- Very rarely in salary negotiation are they negotiating with their own money, which does give you an edge, although some do 'go native' and give you the impression they're paying you out of their own pocket

- Salaries/packages can be more fluid in SME's than in the larger companies with more rigid pay scales/bands

- This particular Case Study is a very rare scenario. In most cases David would have been allowed to settle for his opening price of 65 thousand or even been forced to negotiate down

- Again, watch out for those invitations to negotiate. When the CEO said 'You're sure that would be acceptable to you?' that was a chance to push for more. That the figure was more than acceptable to David isn't the point

- Be alert to the 'buy' signals. When the Chief Buyer said 'We can sort that out at the next stage' that was a signal to David that he was going to *be* at the next stage. This rightly encouraged David to stop selling as a decision to buy, at least until the next stage, had been made. Any further selling on his part could well have encouraged the Chief Buyer to change his mind. Many would-be negotiators have had a job offer in their pocket after 30 minutes (had they but known it) but who, through their inability to read the 'buy' signals have 'over-sold' and thrown it away

Another brief but worthwhile diversion: It's common to get right down to the wire, receive a verbal offer which you accept, with or without negotiating, but then be invited back for an 'informal meeting' with the Head Honcho who gives you a real and unexpected grilling, at the end of which - a rejection. This can be almost as great a shock to the others as it is to you. Sometimes those at the top of the greasy pole like to remind everyone else 'who the real decision maker is around here'. It ain't over 'til it's over.

The role of the 'gate-keeper'

As there are many permutations and variations, and because no two meetings are the same, we can't draw too many hard and fast rules about who, amongst the people you'll be meeting, has the power, the influence and the authority to say 'you're hired'.

But gatekeepers, by definition, don't have it. Gatekeepers are those who, typically, appear early in the process. They'll most likely be the ones who have read your résumé and decided to meet you. They have the power to get you in front of the decision maker and the power to stop you from getting there - they are a filter. Your objective, then, when meeting gatekeepers, is *not* to get the offer, and *not* to negotiate salary, but to ensure that you get to turn up for the next meeting. It's this inability to see the big picture and 'play it long' that causes many sellers to be eliminated after that first meeting. There are two 'pitfalls' that make this happen:

- Pre-emptive and impulsive decision making

- Failure to reassure the gatekeeper

Pre-emptive and impulsive decision-making

We have all applied for jobs, got the meeting with the buyer, had the talks but realized that it isn't the right job for us. A job can be 'wrong' for many reasons and it's no one's 'fault'. That's the way it is. Sometimes we realize this at the first meeting, sometimes not until the offer is made. Often the buyer realizes it before we do. But under the stressful conditions of an interview *we are not always best placed to make a judgment* that 'this is the wrong job for me.' The whole process is a 'fact-finding tour' for both parties. But gatekeepers can deliver up a 'fact' to you at a first meeting, which might make your heart sink, your enthusiasm dim and your performance wane, but which at the next meeting (if only you'd got it) or at the offer stage, turns out to be misleading or untrue. **Case Study 7** demonstrates this:

CASE STUDY 7

Jennifer turned up for a first meeting with a gatekeeper. Preliminary courtesies were exchanged and the gatekeeper did most of the talking, said a few things about the role and then, still early in the meeting, opened at a price:

Gatekeeper: The base salary is 80k plus usual benefits.

Jennifer: Oh - is that base negotiable? That's less than my last salary and I'm not looking to take a drop?

Gatekeeper: No, it is what it is. What *was* your last salary?

Jennifer: 85 - I don't expect you to match that but the closer you could get to it the more comfortable I'd be.

Gatekeeper: Well look, we may be able to do something but let's move on and you tell me something about yourself.

The meeting moved on but things never really recovered after that. Jennifer wasn't invited back. They eventually offered the job to one of Jennifer's competitor's at a base salary of 90k. Not that Jennifer ever knew that.

Case Study 7 highlights a number of classic errors:

- When gatekeepers voluntary open at a price don't 'stick your nose in the trough' and allow yourself to get drawn into a premature negotiation. You want to get to talk to the one holding the purse strings. As a rough guide there are 3 levels at which they can open:

1. High. Higher than your previous package. Well, then you'll be mighty pleased that you dug your heels in and declined to open. So you're delighted but don't let you're body language display that delight. Be inscrutable and say 'Well I don't think we'll be falling out over that so let's carry on talking.' It is after all their opening price so you might want to negotiate on that - *when you have the offer*.

2. This is the dangerous one that Jennifer got. 80 was right on her bottom line (of which more later). It was a 'heart sinker' and it's this one that draws you in. As soon as you start asking questions like 'Is it negotiable?' 'Does it include this?' 'Does it include that?' it's way too late to say

'let's discuss it later'. If she had remained inscrutable, as in 1 above, maintained enthusiasm and said, 'Well, I'm looking for the right role and the package isn't a deal breaker - there's other things I'd take into account.' then she would have stayed in the game.

3. So far below your bottom line you just know it isn't going to happen. In which case you may as well throw your cards on the table and say so. This is a very rare category as it's a complete mismatch so there's been a real misunderstanding somewhere along the track. But it isn't at all dangerous - just deeply, deeply disappointing.

•   Although the buyer had opened, which is good for the seller, Jennifer made the mistake of voluntarily revealing her previous salary by saying 'that's less than my last salary' and then taking a stance that was not in her interests 'and I'm not looking to take a drop.' Taking a stance like that often makes positions become entrenched. Both sides are 'digging in' and the seller invariably loses

- 'Is that base negotiable?' Jennifer shouldn't have asked it at all at this early stage but she also framed the question badly. A closed question like 'Is it negotiable?' is clearly inviting the answer 'No, it isn't' which leaves the seller nowhere to go. An open question 'How negotiable is the package?' strongly implies that it is of course negotiable so how much extra can you find?' Now that's the question to ask *but, ideally, only at the offer stage*

- 'I don't expect you to match that but the closer you could get to it the more comfortable I'd be.' Now that's an *impulsive concession* (Chapter 5) that Jennifer didn't have to make. That invites them to still offer less than her previous salary. No advantage in saying that. When you have an *offer* below your previous package and you think they might have a struggle to match it then *that* can be the time for you to reveal your previous salary / package and say '...the closer you could get to it the more comfortable I'd be.' That's a conciliatory stance that you might have to take

All things considered then **Case Study 7** was a real dog's breakfast. See the whole recruitment process as a courtship between seller and buyer. The more meetings you have the hotter things are getting. At the end of the first meeting the buyer may like you and they want to meet you again. But they have other suitor's they also like and want to meet again so why discuss the price? At the end of the second meeting the buyer may love you, but they may also love one other suitor, so why discuss the price? Your competitors are falling away. At the offer stage the buyer is saying 'I must have *you*.' Then you discuss the pre-nup. Once you've signed on the dotted line it's 'I've got you'. It's too late then.

Pre-emptive and impulsive decision-making is a common error. If you are impatient and impulsive by nature you may take the view that there are certain questions to which you need answers sooner rather than later, on the basis that you don't want to waste your time or theirs. This has a certain superficial logic, but there are 4 reasons for questioning this:

1. **No meeting is a 'waste of time', even if you know you wouldn't take the job if it were offered**. Every meeting is part of your learning curve. You'll need as much experience as you can get of being a seller. It takes about 6 meetings to get up to peak performance. Once you've got 6 under your belt you are then as good as you're going to get. Practice your technique in situations where it may not matter if you screw up - use it as a rehearsal for the main event. These meetings are gold dust. Any chance you get to put yourself in front of a stranger and practice your technique - take it.

2. **Pre-emptive and impulsive decision-making is taken to extremes when sellers decide to turn down first interviews on the basis that 'I'm no longer interested in the job'**. This is

crazy. There are many, many examples of sellers who have bothered to turn up, given a good performance (despite their private ambivalence about the role) *and been offered something better.* If you maintain enthusiasm for the role under discussion then you'll be sending signals that you want to work for the company. That is the *undertow.* It's only then that buyers consider lining you up for something better that they haven't even got around to advertising, *and for which you would have no competition.* If your enthusiasm is visibly waning for the role under discussion, based on some spurious 'fact' that's come your way (see 3 below), then the undertow is that you *don't* want to work for their company. Then you never uncover those hidden gems.

3. **Don't make the mistake of assuming that they even know what their problem is**. The whole process is often an exercise in misunderstanding, miscommunication

and misleading information. Gatekeepers and their decision-making colleagues don't always agree on what they are looking for. The 'problem' can change over the course of the recruitment process. Roles are often re-shaped during the process, to such an extent that the role offered bears little resemblance to the one originally advertised. For better or for worse. Why did they offer the job to another suitor at a higher price and not to Jennifer? Maybe because Jennifer didn't play it long and get them to like her. Maybe because her competitor did. But perhaps because the gatekeeper got it wrong about the price. Simple as that. I've had many clients who have played it long, remained true to their objective and got a written offer with a price tag higher than that put forward by a gatekeeper at the first meeting 3 months earlier. No negotiation even necessary sometimes.

4. **Even if you *know* you don't want the job and even if you *know* you don't**

want to work for the organization then still turn up for that meeting. Why? *Because it can get you to the negotiation table at other organizations*. Every meeting is a networking opportunity. You're making a new personal contact and even if you don't want to sell to them and they don't want to buy from you, they may be able to introduce you to someone else, or give you 'market intelligence' upon which you can act. If you don't show up you never make that kind of luck. You must allow your instincts to tell you when to withdraw from the process with good grace as your reputation is paramount, and you don't want to compromise that. In other words, don't get yourself a reputation as a time waster, particularly in a close knit or insular market place.

Failure to reassure the gatekeeper

The role of the gatekeeper is not an enviable one. Recruiting is not an exact science and we've already seen that 8 out of 10 of the buyers you'll be in front of will have had no training or even experience in the dark arts of selecting round pegs for round holes. Professional capability is on the line here - not just yours but theirs. They all want to keep their job more than they want to give you one, and everyone you meet is in fear of losing their job. Everyone. They might not show it but they are.

Your role is to help them keep their job by encouraging them to make the right decision, which is to select *you* for the next meeting. You achieve this by providing them with evidence that you have what it takes to do the job - we saw in Chapter 3 what this evidence consists of. You have gathered the ammunition and now you have to fire the bullets.

Most often the gatekeeper or first interviewer is accountable to the second or next interviewer. When that first interviewer decides to recommend you they are in effect your ambassador and they'll most likely be asked to *justify* that recommendation. They have to sell you to their colleague or, if it's an agency, they have to sell you to their client. They won't risk doing this unless and until you've reassured them that you won't let them down and have their credibility compromised.

We saw in **Case Study 7** that Jennifer failed to reassure the gatekeeper about the price. But it may not be the price that buyers get confused about. For example, the person who has the problem, and that's often the one with the power to hire you, may believe it *essential* that the right person for the job must have a specific academic qualification, maybe an MBA. The gatekeeper may see this as only a 'desirable' and not a deal breaker if the seller is right in every other respect. Headhunting firms can have interesting and heated debates with their clients on all kinds of issues. So, the gatekeeper has read your résumé, seen that you don't have this 'essential' yet still decides to meet you. They'll then put the 'objection' on the table, *and take ownership of it*; 'Ideally *we* were looking for someone with an MBA and you don't have that - how much of a disadvantage do you think that'll be?' Now this objection can't be insurmountable. If it were then you wouldn't be there. This is a 'cry for help' and you don't help them by criticizing MBA's or by saying ' Hey, you've had my résumé for 3 weeks, you know I don't have an MBA and I've come a long way today, what am I doing here?' That's called shooting the messenger.

The gatekeeper is really saying 'This objection isn't a deal breaker - if it were you wouldn't be here, and personally I don't believe an MBA is essential, but there's a guy further down the track who's got a real issue with it. What ammunition can you give me, to give me the confidence to go into battle for you, because my credibility is on the line?' How you overcome that objection is fully dealt with in 'Winning At Interview'.

---------◆ ◆ ◆ ---------

CHAPTER 5

ASSESSING THE BALANCE OF POWER

Jockeying for position

We've already established that you must approach your meetings with buyers and conduct negotiations with a positive mental attitude - for it is attitude that dictates the balance of power, nothing else, not even the 'reality' of the situation. If you *are* confident and feel powerful then you'll most likely be sending signals of power. Most job hunters feel vulnerable and powerless and so transmit those signals to the buyer, which in turn weakens their negotiating position. But this is an art, not a science and one of the great arts of selling yourself in the jobs market, and negotiating, is to maybe *be* vulnerable and powerless but still be able to send signals of power. Now if you can do that then you have the power. So, the good news is that it doesn't matter a damn who *has* the power - if you make them think you have it, then you have it.

This 'balance of power' is not an overt thing. Buyers are not generally sitting there thinking 'who's got the power, me or you?' It's a subliminal dynamic. Don't confuse power with 'dominance', 'aggression' or 'intimidation'. Assertiveness is good but aggression is always bad. It's folly to try and compensate for a weak hand by being unnaturally forceful. Success lies in knowing how to react with firmness and confidence to specific questions, the answers to which, *and your accompanying body language* give the buyer a pretty clear indication of your self-image and your negotiating strength. But before we go on to look at some examples it's helpful to put all this into some kind of perspective.

The meeting should not be an interrogation, though it might turn into one if you let it. Neither are all buyers devious, conniving, adversarial, underhand nor trying to trick you or plain out to get you. They're simply seeking to find out if you can do the job, whether you will fit in and then agree on a price. And for your part you're not trying to screw them for every dollar, pound, euro or yen you can get.

They may not themselves always understand why they're asking certain questions, but it's your responses that will send either positive or negative signals, on which they will of course base their judgment.

So, how important is money to you?

We saw in **Case Study 2** how Michael's poor response to this question sucked him into a premature discussion on the price. In addition, his weak response that it wasn't the 'be all and end all' gave the impression not just that he had a cavalier approach to money but that he would be a 'soft touch' if it came to salary negotiation - which of course it didn't.

How else, then, might he have chosen to answer the question? Well, those 2 out of ten perceptive and trained interviewers, and remember, those are the one's who understand their problem and have clarity on the kind of person they need to solve it, well, they'll *frame* their questions carefully, and quite deliberately, to see how the seller interprets them and how they run with them. So, if their target is someone for a role that's a real 'profit centre' and they need a person who is by nature entrepreneurial, then they don't mess around. For them the word 'money' triggers 'profit' and they respond accordingly - 'Well, it's really important. The only reason you're in business is to make a profit. And for me it's my raison d'être - it's what I do. But I believe everyone in the company should take that view. We can't lose sight of the profit imperative. For sure we don't have unlimited budgets, and value for money is important for our customers. Give them value for money and they'll most likely stick around.'

'Now that's not a guy like Michael who just turned up to solve *his* problem and get a job with a salary on the end of it. No, here's someone who's turned up to demonstrate how he could make money for *my* company, and that's the only reason we're having this meeting. He's not going to get sucked into a premature salary discussion and he's sent me a strong signal that he won't be a pushover when we do get around to discussing it, which we will - but good, he's my man. I liked you Michael but so long and good luck.'

Many of my clients say to me 'Ok - I get the 'don't discuss the price until you've made the sale' stuff, but how realistic is it - on most occasions you get into that early on in a meeting? My answer is 'yes, but not *always* because the buyers want to discuss it. It's because you get guys like Michael who are not 'in the zone', have only turned up to get a job and at the first mention of money have got their nose in the trough.'

Now don't get paranoid. It's just that smart interviewers will choose their words carefully.

Pre-emptive and impulsive concession giving

You may have to concede on aspects of the TRP at some stage but at all costs resist conceding until the latest possible stage. The buyer may wish to assess by how much you're willing and able to concede at an early stage. Or just mild curiosity on their part can flush it out, as we'll see from **Case Study 8**.

CASE STUDY 8

Frankie had just completed a pensionable engagement in the Army and was unsure about the kind of salary that could be commanded in the private sector as a civilian. At the interview, and not knowing what salary they were expecting to pay, this question was asked:

Buyer: I guess you have a pension from the military?

Frankie: I'm lucky to have a pension yes, which means I don't need to earn as much as some as the other people you're seeing.

Buyer: How much *do* you need?

The buyer may just as well have said 'How *little* do you need?'

Frankie's uncertainty led him into making a preemptive and impulsive concession, which may have turned out to be unnecessary. In so doing he completely eroded his negotiating strength and tipped the balance of power in favor of the buyer. Understandably, and given his uncertainty, he was using his pension as leverage to clinch the offer over his competitors. He did win the offer, but at a salary much lower than his previous service pay. No surprises there. This didn't faze Frankie because 'hey, it's a job and I can use my pension as a top up and still be better off, plus I'm not getting shot at.'

But his tactics were highly questionable. Firstly, there's nothing 'lucky' about having a pension from the military, or any other pension for that matter. Pensions are hard won. Yes, they do give you more flexibility when it comes to choosing a new career. You *can* use it to subsidize another employer's low pay. But that's not what it is *for*. What better offer might he have achieved if he hadn't made that concession? Well, we'll never know for sure but any other income you might have is no one else's business. This is not to say that Frankie should have said that in his reply - responding aggressively doesn't weaken the other party but toughens them up, and if positions become entrenched and confrontational the seller loses. But making unforced concessions also toughens up the other party and weakens your position.

Frankie may well have needed his pension as leverage, not to get the offer but to maybe (and maybe not) concede a little, if necessary, during any later discussions, or ideally after receiving the offer,

How might he have more confidently responded, still maintaining his negotiating strength but without antagonizing the buyer? Why else might the question have been asked? Maybe the buyer wasn't trying to get Frankie on the cheap at all. Some buyers might believe that if you've another source of income then you might not give the job 100% commitment. So Frankie should have removed that fear from their mind: 'Yes, but I need a challenge that requires my total commitment. I'm not interested in something to top up my pension.' This is a robust response but not confrontational. It also neatly makes the point, just in case they *were* looking to get him on the cheap, that, by the same token, he wasn't going to use his hard won pension to top up their low salary.

Impulsive concession giving is a trait often found in those not used to the cut and thrust of negotiation. They believe that if they're accommodating to the buyers then that encourages them to be more giving. This isn't true. They see appeasement as a sign of weakness. It fuels the desire for power and encourages them to be even tougher.

To protect the vulnerable

There are other factors that influence the buyer's perception of the balance of power. I've already said much about your competitors - but what about the buyer's competitors for your services? A vital part of your selling technique, which in turn strengthens your negotiating position, is to resist giving any indication that you're in a weak and vulnerable position. You *are* in a weak and vulnerable position if no other buyers are showing an interest in you. Vulnerability can be cruelly exposed at these meetings. **Case Study 9** will serve as an example:

CASE STUDY 9

Hilary lost her job, took a 3-month sabbatical to re-charge her batteries and had been in the jobs market for 6 months. During that period she had achieved some interviews and one job offer that she'd turned down, as it wasn't the right job. At the time of this interview she didn't have any others lined up.

Buyer: How long have you been unemployed?

Hilary: nine months.

Buyer: How have you been spending your time?

Hilary: Well, I've been job hunting and catching up on those things that always need doing around the house.

Buyer: Wow - nine months is a long time -why haven't you found a job yet?

Hilary: Well, there's blood on the streets out there. There are just too many people chasing too few jobs.

Buyer: Are you talking to any one else?

Hilary: No, it's pretty quiet right now.

All in all this was a weak performance that oozed vulnerability. These responses could not have failed but to give a negative perception of the seller. If Hilary was selling anything at all it was lethargy, apathy and defeatism. And there's no doubt the body language would have been sending those signals. Let's take the questions one at a time:

'How long have you been unemployed?'

At least Hilary's response can be commended for its brevity but too much of that and you end up with an interrogation on your hands. There's something about the word 'unemployed' which, when voiced, carries with it an accusatory tone. There's also something judgmental about the question. All things considered then, the question carries with it a whole lot of baggage that Hilary could well have done without. The question may not have been designed to make her feel vulnerable but that was its effect. Hilary capitulated by simply answering the question without expanding on it in a positive way. The question was inviting a more upbeat response:

' Well, I took a 3 month break to re-charge the batteries so I've been in the market for 6 months. But I sure don't feel as if I'm unemployed. I know now why they say a job hunt is a full time job in itself - there's not enough hours in the day.'

That's a more assertive but not combative response that neatly declines to accept the baggage of the word 'unemployed'. It also negates the buyer's second question and possibly the third question because Hilary had correctly made the distinction between the length of time 'unemployed' and the time job hunting. But let's take the question anyway:

'Wow - nine months is a long time - why haven't you found a job yet?

Blaming the state of the market and the strength of the competition is both predictable and weak. The question is almost inviting an apology for being in the market. It also implies, wrongly, that no one had offered her a job and Hilary, unwisely, didn't refute it.

A more robust approach would have been better:

' Well I'm not looking for just any job. This is a key time for me in my career development and I've got to be as selective as I can about my next role. Interesting things have come up and I was offered a role but at the end of the day I didn't feel it was right for me - and if it's not right for me it's not right for the company.'

Now that keeps the balance of power. It also neatly implies 'I'm not desperate for a job. I've had the courage to turn one down so don't assume I'm going to bite your hand off either.'

'Are you talking to anyone else?'

Or in other words 'are other buyers showing an interest in what you're selling - because if they're not, why am I talking to you?' Hilary felt obliged to say 'No' as she hadn't been to other interviews recently. But that wasn't the question. Others might also have felt obliged to say 'No' because to say otherwise might have indicated a lack of commitment to that particular buyer. But most buyers would see it as negligent for you *not* to be talking to others. Hilary was managing a good campaign and *was* talking to people all the time, but she omitted to say so:

'Sure, I'm networking like crazy. Success is a combination of hard work, timing and a bit of luck.'

All the advantages lie in you being able to say, in effect, 'you bet I am.' It can concentrate their mind to know that other buyers are competing for your services. Your negotiating strength increases if you gently sow the seed that you are in demand.

People you meet, and not just buyers but your network contacts, will be curious about how your job search is progressing. *Your job search is always going well*. Now that means that sometimes you do need to 'talk it up.' It's legitimate to do that. In the world of business it's a given that 'business is always going well' even when it *isn't* going that well. Business people who broadcast that their business is slack may as well call in the receivers. No one wants to hear bad news and bad news travels fast. But enthusiasm is infectious - if you've got it, they'll catch it.

There's another important dimension to this. Your network contacts will only put the effort in if they *see* you leading from the front. You do that by letting them know you are putting in the hard yards and giving your campaign 100%.

Any signal from you that *you're* not taking it seriously and they will disappear like smoke in the wind.

In the great sweep of your campaign the timing of the question 'Are you talking to anyone else?' or 'How's your job search going?' can have real significance. For example, if at a first meeting for the job of your choice this conversation can take place:

Buyer: How's your job search going?

Seller: So far so good. I've got other meetings scheduled and a final interview soon but I've still got to keep my foot on the gas.

Buyer: A final interview soon? Are you likely to have a decision to make before we've had time to go through our procedure?

Seller: I could have that dilemma.

Buyer: Well if that happens don't make a decision without telling me. Keep me in the loop.

Now that is a very strong 'buy' signal. They are clearly indicating 'This has gone well, we believe you're the solution to our problem and we can get our skates on if we think we're in danger of losing you to the competition.' Buyers who may have been dragging their heels for months can be galvanized into action.

Don't allow yourself to be forced to divulge the name of their competitor, unless it's an agency / search firm you trust. You may be talking to another organization that wouldn't want it to be known in the market that they are recruiting. You are selling your integrity and you can often sell that by declining to answer a question.

Revealing the hidden objections

If the 'objection to the sale ' is voiced by the buyer during the meeting this does give you the chance to defend it in a robust and convincing manner. But few buyers have the courage to voice their objection(s). These 'hidden objections' can seriously hamper your chances of reaching the negotiation table. So there's no point in discussing the price until all the objections have been overcome.

Towards the latter stages of a meeting you might want to give the buyers an opportunity, that they might well thank you for, to voice any objections they might be harboring. You do this by asking a straight question. You must give a confident preamble though:

Seller: I've enjoyed our discussion. *I'm* confident about my ability to do it and do it well - but do you have any reservations about my suitability?

Buyer: (After a slight pause) Well I can't make a decision today (you've asked for an opinion not a decision) as I have other people to see but no, I've enjoyed it too (they mirror that back to you) and I've no reservations but let's see how it goes with the other candidates.

That's made it a bit more difficult for them to reject you but of course not impossible.

Alternatively they now raise the hidden objection or come back to an objection you thought you'd put to bed an hour ago. You do your best in the time remaining to reassure them but the bonus is you take it away with you, give it some more thought and in your follow up e-mail maybe reassure them some more.

Some sellers see this as a 'dangerous' question to ask. Their inclination is to get out while they're still in one piece and not stick around to get embroiled in contentious issues. Your confidence to ask the question will be directly related to your perceived ability to deal effectively with whatever objection might be raised. In other words, the more vulnerable you feel the less likely you are to ask it. And if you feel you've made a complete mess of the meeting then you most certainly won't ask it. If you do the buyer will say 'I've got a list as long as you arm - how much time have you got?'

Yet there are two good reasons why, if you feel it's gone well, it's a 'no lose' question for you:

1. If they do voice an objection this is your chance to defend it. If you don't ask the question then they'll still have the objection after you've left.

2. If they don't have one make them say so. Sure, they can still reject you if someone better comes along but that's the way it is.

If for example you'd earlier made an indiscretion and allowed yourself to get drawn into a premature discussion on salary, and mishandled it, their objection may be that you have 'overpriced' yourself. If you encourage them to say so at the end of the meeting then it does give you the opportunity to be more conciliatory and concede a little.

Both hidden and voiced objections can then, if not countered, give the buyer a rationale for either rejecting you or taking a more rigid position when negotiating salary.

Selling your strengths and defending your weaknesses

This critical aspect of assessing the balance of power is more fully covered in 'Winning At Interview' but we must give it a mention here. Although the meeting with the buyer should be more than a question and answer session the strength of your negotiating position (or indeed, whether you reach the negotiation table at all) will depend upon your ability to 'sell' when faced with 'strength highlighting' questions, and your skill in 'defending' when confronted by ' weakness highlighting' questions. Here are just some examples of each:

Strength Highlighting = positive negotiating power

Tell me about yourself

What's your greatest strength?

What's your greatest achievement?

How important is money to you?

Why do you want to work here?

How would you define success?

What can you offer us?

Weakness Highlighting = negative negotiating power

What's your greatest weakness?

What was your biggest mistake?

Why did you leave your last company?

How important is money to you?

Tell me about a time when you've failed at something

Why haven't you found a job yet?

We've already met some of these and, as we now know, 'How important is money to you?' appears in both categories because how you interpret and respond to it decides which category it's in. These (and a lot more) are the questions you must ask yourself before turning up. The strength highlighting questions are not inherently dangerous. They are all 'Tell me why I should hire you?' or 'Tell me why we should get around to negotiating salary?' questions.

They are then all opportunities to *sell*. You're begging for those questions because your responses will win you the prize.

The weakness highlighting questions are altogether more menacing and are essentially 'Why shouldn't I hire you?' or 'Tell me why we *shouldn't* get around to negotiating salary?' questions. Should you be ill prepared to answer these questions then you may as well keep your coat on and fall on your sword.

'Tell me about yourself' is in essence a 'blank check' question but it's alarming how few sellers bother to fill it in. It normally elicits a 30 second poorly conceived and delivered monologue that just withers on the vine. You can't normally sell anything in response to the weakness highlighting questions. These are the 'fast balls' that you need to kill stone dead because the more time you spend answering these the more likely you are to get knocked out of the game.

Excess baggage

There can be negative, and sometimes subliminal, influences on the balance of power that can serve to put you on the back foot. Failure to negotiate can be a consequence of all the 'excess baggage' we take with us to 'interviews' that we wouldn't dream of taking to any other business meeting. This burdensome load comprises a mixed bag of junk - 'job beggar' attitude, low self-esteem and simply being sick to death of the job search being just three of them. This baggage alone is a big enough de-motivator, but we often find, on arriving at the interview, another load waiting for us.

That these meetings never take place on the seller's territory affects the balance of power before the two parties even start talking with each other. On top of that, on arrival, the visible signs of success and wealth can be intimidating. Don't take any of this at face value. See it for the veneer that it is. This is the 'corporate plumage' that serves to entice and ensnare the clients/customers. With few notable exceptions it's not there for you or the others working there.

You may find that the meeting is scheduled to take place on neutral territory e.g. in an hotel. There may be sound reasons for this, but you should at least ask the question 'Why?' Perhaps their premises are totally devoid of 'corporate plumage' or perhaps just a mailing address. Maybe they haven't got around to firing the current jobholder.

Fashions come and go in recruitment. So-called 'stress interviews' used to be in vogue and you might still come across them but unlikely.

Intimidation tactics may be used, such as your being kept waiting beyond the appointed hour, being seated in a chair lower than theirs so they appear to be looming over you, and constant, pre-arranged, interruptions. All of this can, if you let it, upset your equilibrium and make you feel more vulnerable, and we've already seen what vulnerability can do.

Rise above all this nonsense and remember you always have the power of veto i.e. you can terminate these meetings whenever you like. If intimidation tactics are being used you have a choice. You can either terminate the meeting or, if you recognize it for what it is you can stick around to test your performance in the face of naked aggression. But, you might be wise to ask yourself 'If they think it necessary to use these methods to find the right person then what kind of people are they and do they deserve me?

It's all too easy for those less confident to come away from these meetings having left their self-respect behind. This is arguably the worst thing that can happen - it makes rejection pale into insignificance. If you let this happen you'll *never* forget it and it will have an adverse effect on your performance at subsequent interviews. The memory of such an experience becomes yet more 'excess baggage' to carry around.

Your objective in going to the meeting is to either get to the next meeting or get the written offer. Nothing should distract you from this *unless you feel your self-respect slipping away*, in which case you are unlikely to get the offer anyway. You could hang around long enough to ask your 'killer' question. What's the killer question? Always turn up with one of these. This is your nuclear option which rarely if ever will you have to use. This is your weapon of last resort that ensures you leave the meeting with a smile on your face and your head held high. It's best served cold - a calm demeanor and a hint of a smile playing around the edge of your lips. They'll have been drilling down on your résumé, testing it for credibility and asking you some sneaky probing questions. Well, you read their stuff before turning up so do the same e.g. 'Your website and your job ad says you're a dynamic company. How can you demonstrate that dynamism?' Or ' Your ad said this was an "exciting role" - how can you demonstrate that it's exciting?' You don't get to negotiate but what the heck.

Dress for success and strive to impress

A cliché for sure but you don't get a second chance to make a first impression, and first impressions are visual. There's also a strong correlation between dress and performance. If you look good you'll feel good and if you feel good you'll perform well. A confident visual image really can mask your insecurities. A good tip is to spend twice as much money on a suit but have half as many of them. If you can turn up looking as if you already work there you're more likely to end up doing so. You really can't expect to command top dollar if you don't look top dollar, any more than you would get to negotiate a six-figure salary with a five-figure résumé. See expenditure on clothes as an investment - not a cost.

Knowing how to walk into a room with confidence is an art on its own and it's a real advantage to have *presence*, which even some star performers don't have. This is an old one but Winston Churchill once said of a member of the opposition and one time Prime Minister ' An empty taxi pulled up and Clement Atlee got out.'

Ensure that you treat with courtesy *everyone* you meet. In Chapter 4 we saw how important it is to identify the decision maker. Well, sometimes in an organization the real decision maker can be the most unlikely person, at least in a recruitment context. Many sellers have come badly unstuck through their shoddy treatment of the buyer's secretarial staff, often because that's how they treat *their* staff. It doesn't matter a damn that they go into the meeting with the buyer and sell their socks off. The battle was lost in the reception area. It's not unusual for buyers, after you've gone, to ask others what they thought of you. If you omitted to give them the time of day they'll take great pleasure in relaying this back. And, if sellers are miserable and off-hand then those on the receiving end won't even wait to be asked the question.

The Go-Between

In most negotiating situations you'll rarely encounter underhand tactics on the part of buyers. In some situations though their scheming is worthy of an Oscar. One such situation is that of the 'go-between' - a useful little ruse that can really upset the balance of power. Typically, you'd have a meeting with the decision maker. This is the one with the power to hire you and the one who would most likely be your boss. This meeting is productive and the price is not discussed. If all goes well a good rapport is built up, you're enthusiastic about the role and the buyer expresses an interest in offering it to you. In effect the match is being made. At the end of the meeting it's suggested that it might be useful if you had a meeting with A N Other at which the decision maker will not be present. A N Other will be the person designated to discuss the remuneration with you.

This is seemingly an unscheduled meeting and totally spontaneous. It's now that the decision maker becomes the 'go-between' as you are now physically on the move from one office to another. In hushed tones and a 'confide in me' look the go-between says 'Oh - before I introduce you to A N Other what salary/package are you expecting?' Now this can really catch you on the hop. Here you are in no man's land with your 'social hat' on your head. You don't want to negotiate on the hoof but nor do you want to upset your boss by being evasive and he's in a hurry. Before you realize it, and against all your better instincts, you have plucked a figure out of the air.

The go-between now sits you down in a reception area and goes off to confer with A N Other. You've just been mugged.

In the next Chapter we'll look at some strategies for taking evasive action but lengthy sound bites, well articulated and modulated, just don't seem to work in this situation. Best to keep it short and sweet. Look mildly surprised and say 'I've got an open mind - I guess it's "make me an offer" and we'll take it from there.' Short of grabbing you by the throat and rolling around on the floor the go-between has to go away empty handed.

---------◆ ◆ ◆ ---------

CHAPTER 6

STRATEGY AND TACTICS OF NEGOTIATION

Don't discuss the price until you have made the sale

We now know there's a lot more to salary negotiation than simply a conversation about the price. As outlined in previous chapters, your understanding of the 'backdrop' and the 'dynamics' of the situation are critical to your success. We also know that the best time to negotiate salary is after the buyers have decided they want you but before they've got you to sign on that dotted line. This is all very well (and we shall come to it later) but what if the buyer is intent on discussing it *before* that decision is taken?

You may be blissfully unaware of what their intentions are - not just in terms of the package they might offer, but in terms of whether they *expect you*, and indeed themselves, to enter into negotiations. That last point is really quite a critical one, and highlights the importance of your identifying the decision-maker. It's worth remembering that the person that drafted the advertisement may not take an active part in the selection process. Not all interviewers have the *power* to negotiate salary - and not all interviewers have the *inclination* to negotiate, even if they have the power. On the whole negotiators *expect* to negotiate, and are often disappointed if the other party demurs from doing so (**Case Study 2**). In just about any other 'buyer' 'seller' relationship both parties expect to negotiate the price at some point in time. This 'expectation' is not so clearly defined in the jobs market.

If an advertisement has stated that the salary is 'negotiable' then you might be forgiven for believing this to be so. If often turns out though that *that* salary is no more negotiable than any other. Don't take it then as a cast iron indicator of their expectations.

We can then begin to see the potential dangers. Make sure you don't start negotiating too soon with someone who doesn't expect to be negotiating at all, and certainly not within the price range at which you have opened!

So, what was your last salary?

CASE STUDY 10

Carrie had been out of work for some months and had few interviews. She believed her last job had been quite well paid and that she was maybe pricing herself out of the market - although there was no evidence to support this. Her failure to achieve many interviews could not be blamed on past salary, as she had not divulged this.

Carrie was relieved to finally get an interview for an advertised position. Neither party had opened at a price. On arrival the usual pleasantries were exchanged and we'll now pick it up ten minutes into the meeting:

Buyer: What was your last salary?

Carrie: The base salary was 70k. I know that's more than the market rate but I'd need to earn 65k.

Buyer: (3 second pause)

Carrie: Well, 62k minimum

Buyer: Ok - that won't give us a nosebleed

The meeting progressed. Carrie was invited back for a second and final meeting, and was offered the job at 63k. There were no additional benefits. She accepted.

We could argue that as Carrie was offered the job at 1k above her bottom line she came out a 'winner'. But as we shall see there's no 'winners' or 'losers' in salary negotiation. This is why it's inappropriate to speak in terms of 'sides'. That creates an atmosphere that encourages 'positional bargaining', where each 'side' takes an often extreme position and makes concessions to reach a compromise. 'Positional bargaining' can be confrontational and be reduced to a contest of wills. The problem then is that the 'will' of each 'side' to win becomes the big issue at the expense of any desire for both parties to reach a mutually beneficial agreement. In the above Case Study the agreement turned out to be anything but beneficial to either party. So what were the tactical mistakes?

- The buyer was too quick to raise the issue; wrong to raise it in the way it was raised and wrong again not to differentiate between 'salary' and 'package'. It's quite natural for buyers to express curiosity about the price previous buyers have paid for the 'product' - but is it right to do so? Arguably it's no one else's business. The question may be asked, not as a devious means of gaining an advantage at any subsequent negotiating stage, but as an honest attempt to clarify that neither party is wasting the other's time, and that any salary offered would not be appreciably lower than that previously earned by the seller. Such an offer, as we'll see, can lead to retention problems and be more costly to the company in the long run. It doesn't matter all that much what the motive was in this case. It's the effect the question has on the agreement that we need to look at

- As Carrie felt vulnerable she allowed herself to be pressured by the buyer's initial question. This forced her to 'open' with a figure that then became a benchmark. Because the buyer used the word 'salary' and not 'package' Carrie only felt obliged to open at her base salary, omitting to mention that there were 'add-ons' that took the TRP to 75k. *This gave the buyer a false impression of how far Carrie was dropping her price*

- Even though Carrie had not presented the TRP she still felt obliged to apologize for her last salary and linked it to something called the 'market rate'. The 'market rate' is a mysterious term with a somewhat phantom like quality. It makes occasional appearances on the scene. Few people know quite where it comes from and sellers allow it to frighten them to death. The 'market rate' holds no fears for recruitment firms - to them it's a much-loved friend whose transient qualities are most appealing. In a buyers market there's not much work around for agencies and it can be their cash flow that determines the 'market rate'

- Carrie made *two* impulsive concessions. After she opened at 65k the buyer paused for three seconds (try it), deliberately or otherwise. This gave Carrie time to reconsider her opening price, lose faith in it and then make another unforced concession to 62k. They offered 63k so on the base salary alone that pause could have cost Carrie 2k. Silence is a most powerful tool of communication and can be used to great effect by both buyers and sellers

- Carrie's whole strategy, such as it was, may have been based on a false premise, i.e. that her last job had been unusually well paid. Now it either was or it wasn't but it is a mistake to allow this to dictate your strategy. If her previous company was prepared to pay what others would have seen as an excessive package then presumably it benefited it to do so. *Value for money* is an important consideration in salary negotiation, as we will see in the next Case Study

The outcome of this sorry tale is predictable. Carrie found that the duties and responsibilities in her new role were much the same as before. But because she had not herself fully understood the extent of her financial sacrifice her position became impossible, she had no choice but to activate a new job search and get something more equitable. Her company then had to incur the expense of recruiting all over again. Such are the penalties of both parties negotiating a mutually detrimental deal as opposed to a mutually beneficial one.

It's important to understand that in the above Case Study no meaningful negotiation took place at all. For sure, an agreement was reached but through *compliance* rather than negotiation. There are always exceptions but you can't expect to negotiate your salary after committing yourself to an agreed price. Carrie couldn't legitimately go back to them 3 months into the role and saying 'look, I made a mistake. I can't manage on this salary. Once an agreement has been reached a line has been drawn in the sand.

Body talk

Before looking at how Carrie might have dealt with this more effectively we must consider the positive and negative power of body language. As your negotiating strength diminishes in proportion to the vulnerability you display, it doesn't cut it if your voice is delivering the right words but your body is displaying how you *really* feel. This is a dilemma for many would be negotiators who are unable to control their physical, and thus visual reactions when faced, literally, with the $64000 question. Certain questions, and 'What was your last salary?' is one of them, can quite easily short circuit the system - poor negotiators give the impression that all communication between brain and body has ceased. In such a way does the term 'knee jerk reaction' take on much significance.

This in itself is another good reason for always showing up for a meeting - you can never get enough practice at it. The body has an alarming tendency to let us down at the most inconvenient of moments. Emotion, or at least any outward show of it, has no place at the

134

negotiating table. The flicker of a smile or the raising of an eyebrow can speak volumes. So, when faced with the question 'What was your last salary?' your body should not be displaying:

- Fear - 'your question frightens me'

- Aggression - 'your question is impertinent'

- Embarrassment - 'I'm uncomfortable with this question'

- Disdain - 'You think I'm stupid?'

- Incredulity - 'I am from the planet Zog'

It will be displaying these emotions if you:

- Swallow hard

- Lean forward

- Avert your eyes

- Shift backwards

- Move your hands/arms

- Adjust your posture

This is not to suggest that you should sit there and look as if you've just been whacked over the head by a length of four by two. It's really a question of balance - if you remain looking poised and impassive you should be all right. And don't stare them out - you don't want them thinking they're in the presence of a homicidal maniac.

It's time to inject a word of caution. Some sellers are very good at doing what is advocated in the next section. They are cool, calm, collected and measured in their response. Others, in part for the reasons stated above, are better off not even trying it. So don't beat yourself up if you give a straight answer to the question. You have not *failed*. You have simply put yourself in potentially, and only potentially, a weaker bargaining position. And most importantly resist the temptation to *inflate* your last salary. It's wrong to do so. Period.

It must also be reiterated though, that if you happen to be selling 'strong negotiating skills' on your résumé then you'd better not roll over like a pussycat on these salary questions (**Case Study 2**).

An alternative response

In **Case Study 10** the question 'What was your last salary?' could have been dealt with more effectively if Carrie had recognized what was inherently wrong with it and been *prepared* to give a response that addressed those problems. A brief re-cap on what was wrong with the question:

- It was inviting Carrie to open at a price

- The subject was 'salary' and not 'package'

- It was raised too early in the meeting. Carrie had sold very little, the 'match' was nowhere near being made and the buyer could not therefore make the judgment 'I like you'

Let's run through an alternative conversation:

Buyer: What was your last salary?

Carrie: Best to talk about the package as salaries can be misleading (pause for breath). But how about coming back to this later (no pause) it might be better if I find out more and you find out what I've got to offer?

Carrie has now:

- Side-stepped the issue in a reasonable manner

- Not opened at a price

- Made the distinction between 'salary' and 'package'

- Bought time to sell herself and 'make the match'

- Indicated that she's not vulnerable or a pushover

- Implied that she will answer the question later (which she may)

- Tempted the buyer to say 'Sure, what have you got to offer? Now that is saying 'Why should I hire you?' and *not* 'How much are you going to cost me?'

If you were to get them to agree to delay this for only an hour then you're in a stronger position to 'open', if you feel you have to, because you've had another hour to make the match and get them to like you.

Interestingly, the odds are very high that if you get it delayed they *don't* come back to it later, which is even better.

The structure and terminology of the above response is crucial so let's dissect it:

'Best to talk about the package as salaries can be misleading'. As we know an important distinction yet benign in its delivery. No one baulks at that. This is why you can and should pause for breath as you won't get an interruption and you need that air for the rest of the response:

'But how about coming back to this later' *Never* say 'I'd rather discuss this later' because an 'enforcer' will be thinking 'Well *I'd* rather discuss it now and it's my show so we're going to discuss it' In such ways do positions become entrenched! Try to get the buyer to *agree* to it 'But how about...' no pause now because an 'enforcer' will interrupt by saying 'Well we could but I don't want to waste your time so let's do it now', which paints you into a corner. So straight on to 'It might be better if I find out more and you find out what I've got to offer?' Our enforcer will most likely seize on this by saying 'Ok - what have you got to offer?'

But let's make it tougher. Say you give that neat 3-part sound bite but they *still* don't buy it. A common excuse for not delaying the discussion, and it's not an unreasonable one, is when they say 'Well, we could come back to it later but I don't want to waste your time by going through this process and then find out that we can't afford you.' Now if you're not ready for that you'll fold and open. But if you're prepared you just have to say 'Well, if that happens I won't feel I've wasted my time (don't worry, not a problem for me) but I don't want to waste your time (your problem then) what package are you offering? (your problem so you open). Now the buyer has no option but to back off or open.

Now let's follow this through because there's a potential danger in encouraging the buyer to open, because you don't know what figure they'll come up with. We first met this in **Case**

Study 7 but it's worthy of a re-visit. As a rough guide, there are three levels at which they can open:

1. High. Higher than your last package. Well, now you'll sure be pleased that *you* didn't open. But don't let that body language display your delight. Remain inscrutable and say ' Well, that won't be a problem so let's carry on.' That's not to say you won't negotiate later on - it is after all their opening price. That's just saying 'it won't be a deal breaker.'

2. They open so far below your 'bottom line' (of which more later) that you know that agreement will never be reached. You may as well throw your cards on the table and say so. No point in you sticking around. Now this is a complete 'mismatch', which is extremely rare. This isn't the dangerous one - it's just deeply disappointing.

3. This is the dangerous one where they open around your bottom line. It is disappointing but not so disappointing that you'll throw your cards on the table. This may be their 'true' figure or they may be 'flying a kite' (of which more later). Either way the mistake now would be to 'stick your nose in the trough' and start asking questions about it. As soon as you start asking questions such as 'Does it include this or that?' or 'Is it negotiable?' then it's too late to say 'I don't want to talk about it' because of course, you're already talking about it.

Should they open at 3 above then stay in the game by saying ' Well, that won't be a problem so let's carry on.' Whether it will be a problem further down the line is neither here nor there. You don't need to find that out now. Maintain your enthusiasm and carry on selling - get them to like you, then you get them to love you, then get them to want you. Allow yourself to get sucked into a premature discussion on the price now and most likely you won't get to the offer, your enthusiasm will be visibly waning so they won't be considering you for a better role that they haven't got around to advertising, and for which you would have no competitors. If you stay in the game and win the offer a couple of months down the track it's more negotiable then than it is now. Also, many sellers have kept their eyes on the prize, despite a sinking heart, only to discover, surprise, surprise, that the package offered is actually a damn sight better than the one indicated at that first meeting two months earlier.

These evasive tactics may not sit well with you in cold print but when delivered in the right way in a meeting they get you respect. Also remember you're not doing this for selfish reasons. You want the buyer to make the right decision and that means helping them to ask the right questions in the right way and at the right time.

What salary are you seeking (and are you worth it?)?

There's nothing impertinent about this question. As in any other market the buyer has an absolute right to know what price you put on your services, but very rarely in business is the price set in stone - it depends on the work to be done and how can you cost it out until you know that?

CASE STUDY 11

Matt had a good job but felt that his career was flat lining. His TRP was 120k. Through good networking he was getting meetings and buyers generally were showing an interest in him. This particular meeting was arranged via a brief telephone call with no indication given about their needs or the price. So Matt was in a strong position - he had a good job and almost certainly had no competition. He was not vulnerable and unlikely then to display vulnerability at the meeting. He met the boss who was also the decision maker and not a gatekeeper. The price was raised early on:

Buyer: What salary are you looking for?

Matt: I'm looking to improve on my present position. To do that I'd need something like 130k to 135k. But that's not my only consideration - career development is my main priority.

Buyer: Are you worth 135k?

Matt: Yes, *I* think so.

Buyer: All right - tell me why?

At least that last question gave Matt the chance to move away from the remuneration topic *and sell something*. But because there was little clarity on their needs he wasn't sure he was selling the right things. For all he knew he was selling irrelevancies - and all with a 135k price tag. There was no offer and no feedback so we can't assume that the price was the deciding factor. But it was unlikely that it did him any favors. What were the tactical errors?

- 'I'm looking to improve on my present position'. This is where an enforcer would interrupt with 'What is your present salary?' There was no advantage to be gained in making that statement

- 'To do that I'd need something like 130k to 135k'. Instant confusion. Don't use vague words like 'something'. Be clear about whether that means 'salary' or 'package'. Matt, unknowingly, could have priced himself out of contention

- 'But that's not my only consideration...' In itself not a bad thing to say, as we'll see later, but by now the damage has most probably already been done

- 'Are you worth 135k?' 'Yes, *I* think so'. The emphasis on the word '*I*' implies that others might think he *isn't* worth it and the word 'think' could scream self-doubt. Alternatively the phrase '*I* think so' could come across as arrogant if poorly modulated

So Matt, paradoxically, could have become a victim of his own *invulnerability*. He may well have thought 'Ok - you want to discuss the price now then let's get on with it.' Yes, sellers can also be enforcers and although this meeting didn't become confrontational it could have done. When it comes down to it we are only worth what the buyer is prepared to pay so a question like 'Are you worth 135k?' does if anything invite a more confident and robust answer as in 'Well, I believe I'm *worth* more than that but I've got to be realistic and for that *package* I'm great value for money.'

Now that not only introduces the word 'package', which could have prevented any confusion, but it also introduces the important concept of *value for money.* It's a good idea to introduce this at key moments in the process, especially when buyers are 'digging their heels in' and showing reluctance to meet your price. In using the term 'value for money' you, the seller, are making a direct connection between the 'price' and the 'performance'. It's obvious that the buyer may be paying two people identical packages but be getting better results from one of them, and that's the one who represents better value for money.

Options for 'opening'

It would be too easy, too simplistic and unhelpful to suggest that the seller should *never* open at a price. The 'dynamics', the 'backdrop' and that all important chemistry and rapport you have, or don't have, with the buyer have a great influence on your choice of strategy.

There's no sense at all in your leaving a meeting having refused to divulge your salary expectations and forcing the buyer to climbdown. That could be winning the battle but losing the war. So you must turn up having thought about your 'opening strategy' should you decide not to go for the delaying option (**Case Study 10**). To prepare for this there are 3 levels of remuneration you need to think about, *and they can all change depending on the scenario:*

1. **Your bottom line.** This, by definition, is the lowest you can and would accept for what hopefully in every other respect is the right job. How might this change? Well, if you need to get a job quickly and don't have the financial resources to sustain a lengthy job search then it might be less than your last TRP, even if you're seeking a similar role in the same sector. It may be lower, or possibly higher, if you are changing career. If you believe, rightly or wrongly, that you've undersold yourself previously and think this is your opportunity to remedy that, then it

would be higher than your last TRP. It may change as your job search campaign unfolds. You can perhaps be a bit more 'bullish' at the start of your job search and pitch it quite high, but if your campaign doesn't go too well you might have to lower it. Location can also be a deciding factor - for an easier commute you may think it well worth dropping the price. *But you need to know where it is at any given moment.*

2. **Your Settlement Price.** This is the level, above your bottom line, at which you would be prepared to settle. This could be described as 'happiness' (there's nothing sophisticated about this exercise). You know it when you see it. This is what you believe to be a fair and equitable price for the work they want you to do. In accepting this you wouldn't feel that you'd undersold or oversold yourself. You would not feel that the buyer was taking advantage of you.

3. **Your Opening Price.** This is the level, above your settlement price, at which you would choose to open. The golden rule is that you never open at the price at which you would be prepared to settle (2 above). Should you do so then at best that's where you would end up settling, but more likely below it. There are always exceptions to the rule. There are occasions when the seller has opened at their settlement price and the buyer has offered more, but don't count on that happening.

We've addressed the issue of vulnerability before but we must now briefly return to it. Those who are desperate for a job will make a huge, often unnecessary, impulsive concession and *open at their bottom line;* 'Well, the *least* I'd be able to accept would be...' The least is now exactly what they'll get, if they get anything at all. This is clearly crazy but when you really need a job you may be so desperate not to oversell yourself that you undersell yourself unnecessarily.

Well, this now begs the question 'Ok - how high above my settlement price do I open?' There's no meaningful straight answer to this. If it were as simple as saying 'Always open at x% above your settlement price then negotiation would be a science not an art.

Failure to think about this beforehand leads sellers into opening above their bottom line but *below* their settlement price. This means they now have to *negotiate up* to 'happiness', which is of course quite possible to achieve. Most likely though the seller will settle at the offer price and not negotiate at all because ' Well, it's not great but it's above my bottom line.'

Another, very common, scenario is where the seller opens above their settlement price (rightly) *but below what should have been their opening price.* This elicits the response ' Well that won't be a problem for us.' This leaves the seller thinking 'I've still opened too low - what other price, higher than that, and if only I'd had the courage to ask for it, wouldn't have been a problem for them either?' The seller is unlikely to ever discover that. Now that's not so bad because the seller has now got 'happiness + so that's more than equitable and greed must not overtake need.

A better strategy is to 'fly a kite' and open at a price that you think might just give them a bit of a problem. This means you must strike a balance between stating a price that should be within the realms of possibility but not one so outrageous that the buyers are now rolling around on the carpet laughing their head off and shouting out 'What color is the sky in your world?' So, as long as you don't overdo it this is a sound strategy with three advantages:

1. You get more respect from buyers if you put a high, even deliberately *too* high, a price on your talents. Many sellers open so low that the buyer's enthusiasm for carrying on the meeting diminishes 'you can't be that good if that's all you think you're worth.' Flying the kite' does retain their interest. Whether they can afford your price or be willing to pay it is beside the point. They now know that if they are to get you then some hard bargaining

may have to be done to knock your price down.

2. It's much easier for you, the seller, to negotiate *down* than to negotiate *up*. Easier for you, if you have to, to *concede* things to the buyer.

3. You can flush the buyer out into revealing their *top* price.

CASE STUDY 12

Steve attended a final interview for a good job. Their needs had been discussed and he had sold himself very well. 100 people had applied for the job, 10 had been selected for interview, seven had been eliminated which left three, including Steve, competing with each other. The chances were then that *all three* could have done the job and done it well. The chances were also high that 20 of the original 100 could have done the job well but 10 of them had lousy résumés so didn't make it to the first interview. He'd been asked to 'open' at the first interview but, unlike the seven who had been eliminated, had successfully got it put on the 'back-burner'. Steve was unemployed and had no other offers pending.

Buyer: Give me some feedback Steve - would you accept this if we offered it to you?

Steve: On the basis of what we've discussed I'm really enthusiastic. How soon could you get a written offer to me, and how soon after that would you need my response?

Buyer: Ah - well we haven't quite reached that stage. I was just trying to gauge your level of interest.

Steve: Oh - well, I want this - I know I can do a good job for you.

Buyer: I guess we need to talk money. What kind of salary are you looking for?

Steve: I've pretty much an open mind on that, and it's the overall package that's important. It's tricky too because I don't want to undersell or oversell myself but I guess I'd be looking at a base salary of 120k plus usual benefits.

Buyer: (sharp intake of breath) - That base is a bit of a stretch for us.

Steve: Well there's the danger, I've just oversold myself! What did you have in mind?

Buyer: The most we could offer on the base is 110k

Steve: Well that's not going to be a deal breaker. I'm looking for the right role and I think this is it so I'm happy to proceed.

Learning points from **Case Study 12**:

- Steve rightly tried to 'close it down' in response to the first question (**Case Study 3**) but it didn't work - no problem

- Steve responded well by saying 'I want this - I know I can do a good job for you.' Very few sellers seize the opportunity to say 'I want this job' but saying you want it can get you the offer. Why? In a buyer's market they have an embarrassment of riches. The three on that short list were all top quality and that's when buyers have a sometimes-heated debate. If they had three jobs to offer they'd take all three. If they find it tough to choose then psychologically they're likely to offer it to the one who *said* they wanted it

- Before giving them his opening price Steve threw in a few 'caveats'. Now the caveats are important because they take the sting out of the opening price and they gave Steve somewhere to retreat to when required. Having an open mind is a virtue and a good signal to send, as it tells the buyer that there's room for maneuver. *They* are now more likely to have an open mind. Note how Steve also stated that the 'overall package' was important, again indicating room for maneuver on the base salary. But the caveat 'It's tricky too because I don't want to undersell or oversell myself' is neat because Steve knows full well that he's now going to quite deliberately oversell himself

- As expected, the buyer was taken aback by Steve's opening price and in effect said 'we can't go that high.' That was Steve's chance, and he seized it, to retreat back to his caveat and in effect say 'well there you go - I've gone and done it - how high *can* you go?' To save any further embarrassment the buyer then opened at top price ' the *most* we could offer on the base is 110k.' And then Steve reeled the kite in by making the right conciliatory noises ' 'Well that's not going to be a deal breaker. I'm looking for the right role and I think this is it so I'm happy to proceed'

- As Steve was unemployed and had no further offers pending he *was* quite vulnerable but had the chutzpah to send signals of power (Chapter 5)

- As this was the end of the final meeting Steve knew that he'd got them to make the judgment 'We love you' so if the price was going to be discussed before the written offer, which it was, then he was in a much stronger position to discuss it now than at the first meeting when at best they only 'liked him.' He *could* have still declined to open and given a more robust response such as ' I have an open mind. I believe I'm right for this role. If you think I'm right then make me an offer an we'll take it from there.' And nothing wrong with that but always put trust in your instincts in these situations, as these can be fine judgment calls. But if you hadn't thought about those 3 levels of remuneration before turning up then you'll most likely be all over the place.

That's where the money is

Logic tells us that if either party is going to open then it's easier for the buyer to do it because they, after all, have got the money and you may have little or no experience of the market. You'll be rusty because you don't job hunt on a regular basis. Now this is the only time in the job search process where ignorance can be an advantage for you. You can, in response to the question 'What salary are you seeking?' look mildly surprised and play the 'green card': 'Well, I've got an open mind. I'm looking for the right role and that decision won't be made on the package alone. And it's tricky as I haven't been in the market for a while so I don't feel I've got a handle on the market rate. I was hoping you would give me a steer on that. What kind of package are you thinking of?' And yes, you can use that mysterious term 'the market rate' to *your* advantage.

An alternative gambit to put them off the scent would be to say, and assuming this is a well established company with well defined pay scales, 'Tricky for me to know where to pitch it. I wouldn't expect any more or less than other people at the same level. How do you decide on remuneration in your company?' They should then be able to say something meaningful to you and this would give you the opportunity to say 'What value have you put on this role?' If given a range then a positive response is to say 'Ideally I would be looking at the upper end of that.'

Job evaluation or person evaluation?

Establishing *how* they decide on remuneration, ideally before you show up for the meeting, is important because organizations adopt different methods (assuming they have a method at all)

159

and some are more rigid than others. As a general rule the more flexible their method the more freedom you will have to negotiate.

In Chapter 3 we asked the question 'What are you selling?' But another valid question is 'What are they buying?' Are they buying a person to fit an already well-defined role *upon which they have already placed a value?* Or are they buying a person with a combination of skills, capabilities or 'competencies' who can be used more flexibly within the organization? It's important not to see these two things as necessarily mutually exclusive - in some organizations one method may be used to complement the other.

The former method 'job evaluation', has been how many large, often government/public sector organizations have used to decide upon what they are going to pay their people. Such organizations have 'fixed' jobs with a clearly defined purpose and which require a non-variable range of skills. Jobs are evaluated in terms of their relative importance to the organization and, as a result, to each other. In large organizations, job evaluation is cumbersome and more useful as a means of complying with equality legislation than as a means of rewarding individual talent, performance and potential.

Increasingly, and this is good news for those preferring individual pay bargaining over collective pay bargaining, these organizations are finding job evaluation, on its own, ineffective because its inherent lack of flexibility is out of step with the fast changing needs of the 21st century. We saw in **Case Study 5** how Carly was able to negotiate a good deal by selling a talent/experience that wasn't actually required for the role under discussion. This is because they were a young, ambitious company going through continuous change and expansion. They were flexible enough to respond positively to her overtures. In a more traditional, larger, well established organization that may not have been possible. It would have been a case of 'If we don't need that skill for this job then we can't buy it.'

Job evaluation per se does not fit the increasing trend for organizations to be less hierarchical, receptive to change, more 'project based', reliant on the flexible use of employees' knowledge and cognizance of individual performance.

Before going to any meeting then you must ask yourself 'what type of organization is this?'

- Government/public or private sector

- Large, medium or small sized? As defined by staff numbers

- Does it have an HR department?

- What is its culture? Not always easy to define but it can be identified in part by its *attitude* towards its people, the 'outside world' and its own raison d'être. Your knowledge of this is likely to be limited unless you know someone within the organization who can answer this question for you

- Is it fast moving? Does it have to react quickly to changing events e.g. market forces? Or does its fundamental role change little over time? Does it have a reputation for hiring top talent?

Considering the written offer

It's not unknown to have a written offer put in front of you at a final meeting and for them to expect you to sign it there and then. Never allow yourself to be steamrollered into making such a decision. Insist on taking it away so that you can review it in your own time. This is one of the most important decisions you'll ever have to make, and not just financially. You will need to think about it in career development terms and unless you have no family responsibilities this is not normally a decision to be taken alone.

Is this your first offer, your only offer, your 1st choice or do you have something better stuck in the pipeline? Is this the time to ring them up and ask if they can speed things up? You should have already clarified when the company making the offer need a response from you, and if you have been having prolonged discussions with another company it is only courteous to give them the chance to move things along if they can but do not play one off against the other. You must act with probity at all times. To do otherwise is wrong and these things can come back and bite you in your next job search, if not sooner. And you don't want to get a bad reputation in the market.

Keep the news of your offer to yourself for now, unless you want to seek wise counsel from a network contact. If you let it be prematurely known in the market and to your contacts that you have an offer it can cause confusion and embarrassment if it were to fall through at the last minute. Once the deal is done and you are home and dry it is then essential that you tell the good news to everyone who has helped you in your campaign. Don't leave anyone swinging in the breeze.

There are a number of key questions to address:

- **Is it the job you *want* or the only job you think you can get?** You may find that you're having to compromise on something, e.g. travelling distance to and from the place of work. If so, then ask yourself if it's worth it. Negotiating a more reasonable financial package, however attractive, can, for some, never really compensate for the stress and strain of making an intolerable journey twice a day. Is it possible to work from home for part of the week? If so, then maybe they haven't considered that as an option and *that* may be negotiable. Is it a five-day week job? If you can negotiate 4 days then that might compensate for a drop in salary/package. It's easy to see already that you can be quite creative in your thinking. This also illustrates the importance of leaving all this to the written offer stage. These things are rarely negotiable during the selection/recruitment process

- **If you have secured this offer from a position of unemployment then a useful 'litmus test' is to ask yourself 'If I'd been in work and *not* job hunting, would I have accepted this offer if they had approached me?** If it wouldn't have attracted you from a position of relative strength then what's the logic of accepting it now? It's understood that there may in reality have been valid reasons why you may *not* have given up your previous job and joined them - that doesn't make it a bad offer. It's also understood that the logic of taking it now might be that it's your only offer, it's taken you 6 months to get it, and you don't have any money. That's sometimes how it is. But remember that you are only as good as your last job and only as good as your last paycheck. This job will be in pole position on your résumé for the *next* time you're in the market. A gloomy thought but don't expect this job to last you as long as your last one

- **Are you compromising on the number of day's vacation?** Some sellers have been able to negotiate on that if the buyer is unable to move on the package. In other organizations it's non-negotiable

- **Have they said when the package will be reviewed?** You may want to get that written into the contract. Ok - a review is only a review, and the guy promising you a review in 6 months time might not be even around to review it. And of course the package you want reviewed in 6 months time is the one you're about to negotiate, not the one on the table. But better to get it in writing if you can

- **Try to be objective when reviewing the offer.** It's easy to kid yourself that the offer is better than it really is. Reluctance to enter negotiations and a natural desire to escape the tyranny of the job search both play a part here

- **What are they asking you to *do* for the money on offer?** Is it a fair day's work for a fair day's pay? Is it *equitable*? Where does it sit on your 'options for opening' (the bottom line, settlement price, opening price)?

- **Are the responsibilities more onerous than before and is this reflected in the price?**

- **Look again at what you've sold.** Is the buyer getting additional skills/talents (not used and therefore not paid for in your previous job)? This might be your 'added value' so why not put a price on it?

- **Have they got the job description right or are you able to re-shape the role to fit your skills/talents?** Are you able to take on another responsibility that dovetails neatly into the role? This might even obviate the need for them to pay someone else to do it - freeing up extra cash for you. Again, you wouldn't have been in a strong position to float these ideas at an earlier stage - only when you feel that you fully understand the nature of their problem. Negotiating your salary/package is rarely about you getting something for nothing. You may have to give something in return for them to justify to others in the organization why they are paying you more. You may have to help them to set a precedent

- **Is the package *performance related* and are their expectations reasonable and achievable?** Have you been given the opportunity to talk to others doing the same job in the organization?

- **If one of the things you are selling is your contacts, i.e. your ability to introduce new clients/customers to the buyer, especially if it would induce them to forsake competing buyers, are they offering a fair and reasonable reward for this?** It may be possible for you to extrapolate some figures based on the likely increased revenue you can bring. They won't pay for this in advance but you may be able to strike a deal based on projected results. Just try negotiating *that* after you've accepted the job and delivered up those clients!

- **If the job is good but their TRP compares *unfavorably* to your expectations (e.g. above your bottom line but below your settlement price) then you need to give serious thought to**

the point(s) on which to negotiate. The closer it is to your bottom line then more likely that you'll need to negotiate on the base salary. If you are taking a drop then *this* is the best time to tell them ' I don't expect you to match my last package (that may be an unnecessary impulsive concession but could equally be a useful 'olive branch') but the closer you can get to it the more comfortable I'd be - you're only as good as your last pay check' can be a good way of putting it to the buyer. A good organization wouldn't be happy knowing that you were taking a drop and they would want to get as close as they can to your previous package, to ensure that you're more likely to stick around. We saw earlier that it's not as easy as you might think to convince a buyer to pay you *less* than you were previously earning on the basis that the job won't stretch you, you won't adjust to earning less and will leave within a few months. That's very frustrating for those who genuinely want to change career and/or 'downsize'

- **Has the buyer 'over priced' the job?** This might seem an odd question to ask. You might assume that in making such an offer the buyer(s) would have asked themselves the question 'Can we afford it?' It's best to assume nothing. There are circumstances e.g. if they've competed for you with another buyer, that their need to 'win you' may have outweighed the financial consideration and this sudden rush of blood to the head may not be in your long term interests. So, just occasionally you may have to ask the question for them. This is not about your taking them for as much money as you can get but your *securing the best deal they can reasonably afford.* If six months down the track they discover they can't afford you then you could be in the market again, with a previous price tag that no one else can afford either

- If the job is good and their package compares *favorably* to your 'options for opening' e.g. between your settlement price and your opening price you may not feel that you want to negotiate at all, and you may not. But it is after all an *offer*, which you can accept, decline or discuss

Considering your leverage and the 'nuclear option'

Before posing to the buyer the question 'How negotiable is the package?' you need to think about how they might react. It is most unlikely that they'd respond by saying 'It's not negotiable at all and because you've asked that we want our offer back.' The worst-case scenario (unless you were unnecessarily heavy-handed in asking your question) is 'It is what it is, we've done our best and can't go higher.' Now, it's essential that you decide what *your* reaction to that will be *before* you ask the question. Will you accept or decline the offer if they can't move on the price? It is now that you must consider your *leverage* and overall position.

- **How urgent is their need?** If it's taken them some time to find the right person i.e. you, and they need to get you in place quickly then the balance of power shifts in your favor

- **How rare are your talents in the market place?** If they could just pick up the phone, ring an agency and get them to provide someone then there's no leverage to be had here. This clearly isn't their preferred option though as they would have done it that way from the outset

- **Do you have competition?** Maybe you never did have competition in which case you always had that leverage. You have the written offer and if you did have competitors you've eliminated them, so now you have that leverage. Bear in mind that if the buyer is sensible they may still have their '2nd choice' candidate waiting in the wings if the deal with you falls through so it pays not to be 'cavalier' or over-confident. And of course, you might *be* their 2nd choice

- **Are they fully aware of your previous salary/package?** If not then they can make no comparisons between their offer and your last price. If you were earning more in your last job and they don't know it then this might be the time to tell them:' The closer you could get to my previous package the more comfortable I'd feel.' If they know they've already offered you more than you were previously earning then they'll question your reason for wanting more and you must question it too. But it might be that you were seriously underselling yourself last time and you don't want to do it this time

- **Do you have any other offers?** Perhaps not on the table but maybe on the horizon? During this period of deliberation you should be alerting other buyers that you have an offer on the way. This is where your investment in a planned job search campaign really pays dividends. If you've attacked the market thoroughly you might be able to speed up the other buyers who might have been dragging their heels. Knowing they could be within days or hours of losing you can really galvanize them into action. To them, the offer that you have is vindication of your sales pitch - you *are* worth buying! Alternatively, some of them may show benign indifference to your 'predicament'. No matter. If they are indifferent now how indifferent were they before you alerted them? This action on your part can sure clear out that old broom cupboard of dead and dying job applications

• **What is in the mind of the buyer?** You've met the people and the personalities and should have some understanding of the way they think. Faced with the question 'How negotiable is the package?' they will need to consider their position and your leverage as above. They should be thinking:

1. Have we made a fair offer and could we improve it even if we want to?

2. What's the downside for us if we don't improve it? Would the seller decline and where would that leave us?

3. How can the seller justify a higher package?

4. How can we justify it to others in the company?

5. Is there anyone else who can do the job?

6. Does the seller have other offers - how vulnerable are they? Would they accept our offer as it stands?

The 'nuclear option' is for you to turn the offer down without having entered into negotiations. Why would you want to do this?

- You're definitely going to accept a better offer and you would be wasting the time of this buyer if you were to embark on a negotiating process

- You're about to accept a better offer but would seriously consider an improved offer from the one you turn down. Going nuclear is an expression of power on your part that leaves them in no doubt where you stand

- You have no other offers, are running out of money and feel they're seriously undervaluing you. But you're really hooked on the joys of grandstanding and brinkmanship. Best you go get some counseling.

CHAPTER 7

NEGOTIATING FROM WITHIN

Gently does it

There's no doubt that it's easier to negotiate the salary/package on first joining an organization than it is to re-negotiate on remuneration from within. Changing from one employer to another is where the real quantum leaps are made. This emphasizes the importance of striking the best deal before joining - it sets a benchmark for all that might follow.

No point now in your hedging about your present salary. They know exactly what you are earning. As we saw in the earlier chapters, overcoming your natural reluctance to negotiate is half the battle. This reluctance may be no less real when you're on the inside. But again, it's helpful to ask the question 'why?' The answer is still *fear*, *vulnerability* and *ignorance*, but the underlying reasons for this are, in part, subtly different. When considering whether to re-negotiate your fear cannot be that they won't offer you the job, for you already have it. Your vulnerability cannot be the result of them perceiving you as a 'job beggar' for even if you were one you are not one now.

Much of your reluctance may still be the result of your ignorance of the way in which to go about it, and understandably so, for by its very nature it is not a skill we utilize on a regular basis. Could your fear be based on the idea that that they might decide to dispense with your services altogether if you ask for an increase, or that such an action might cause you to become 'persona non grata' and relegated to some backwater in the organization? Quite possibly, but the danger of this happening is not a very real one. However, if, and without any warning, you were to go charging into someone's office saying 'I need more money - give me some now or I'm leaving' then the response would be predictable. *No one* is indispensable.

Even if your role were a pivotal one you'd find that in the face of such a threat they would rather totally screw themselves up than accede to your demand - the question of whether they could or could not afford it wouldn't even enter the frame. You might feel that no rational person would ever consider making such a crass approach and yet it happens. It happens through their failure to *timely communicate* their dissatisfaction to those with the power to do something about it. They allow their emotions to build up until they finally feel compelled to communicate but in the form of issuing an ultimatum - and then it's often too late.

Adopting the right attitude is as fundamental to your success here as it is when negotiating from the outside. The wrong attitude sends the wrong signals and it's perhaps your fear of sending the wrong signals that stops you from re-negotiating. Beware of sending signals that say:

- **I am dissatisfied.** A dissatisfied person will most likely be unhappy and therefore ineffective in the role. If, over a period of time, and as a pre-cursor to re-negotiation, you display a negative attitude then this will detract from, rather than enhance, your case.

You'll send these signals if you are: disruptive/uncommunicative/unhelpful/sullen moody/complaining/uncooperative/unprofess ional or aggressive. The build up to the negotiation, and in terms of time we could be talking about 3-6 months, is of prime importance. Asking for a raise is doomed to failure if done on the spur of the moment, at, say, the six-monthly or yearly appraisal meeting. The groundwork has to be laid over a lengthy period, during which your attitude and performance must be beyond reproach - don't give them the leverage to say 'no'. If you display any negative traits then you may find that over a period of time certain responsibilities are actually taken away from you and given to others - thus enhancing *their* case to re-negotiate *their* salaries

- **I am moving the goal posts**. Before agreeing to take the job on you negotiated (didn't you?) a deal that was *mutually beneficial to both parties*. Presumably you were then satisfied with the remuneration offered for your skills, experience etc. *If nothing has changed* in the interim then your grounds for re-negotiating an increase over the rate of inflation and perhaps any previously agreed incremental payments will be slim to none, and attempting to move the goal-posts after the game has started won't endear you to many. In these circumstances your only grounds for re-negotiating might be if it subsequently became apparent to you that others were being paid more for doing the same job. Even then, just as buyers shouldn't peg your salary at the level of others who failed to negotiate, your right to fly on the coat tails of those who did take advantage of the negotiating window is a dubious one

- **I am a troublemaker** Because recruitment is an art and not a science the wrong people are occasionally offered jobs and the 'Trojan horse' is a recruiter's worst nightmare. This is someone who during the selection process exhibits all the right qualities but on joining the organization whips off the mantle to reveal 'the monster from outer space.' Having a Trojan horse in the organization can be every bit as bad as having a virus in your computer system. Your timing is then an important factor. It's no good attempting to re-negotiate before those with whom you need to deal have become comfortable with having you around. Relationship building is a necessary precursor to negotiating from within - and that can take time. You won't always have that time because these days' people come and go with alarming rapidity.

Anticipating their objections

Your strategy should be based on the assumption that if you ask for a raise your employer will say 'no'. You will then need to consider all the possible reasons for their giving a negative response and devise ways of countering them. If you can't do so then arguably you don't deserve one. There's a great deal of difference between *wanting* more money, *needing* more money and *deserving* more money.

If you simply want more, then this is unlikely to get you anywhere - after all, that makes you no different from any one else. If your demands are based purely on need then it's unfortunate but 'hard luck stories' don't cut much ice and, again, although it might make you different from some of your contemporaries it won't from most of them. Deserving more money is the foundation on which your claim must be based. If you can justify (which you will surely be asked to do) your reasons for seeking more then that would enhance your case greatly. We'll look at the possible justifications later but let's firstly cast an eye over some of the objections that might be raised:

'We can't afford it'

Make it your business to establish the financial health of the organization before entering into any negotiations. If you haven't done your homework then when this objection is raised you'll be unable to make meaningful noises about after tax profits, share dividends and not least the increased compensation awarded to directors. Should you be actually *talking* to one of those directors then you may need to display some tact on that last point.

Much of the information you will need will be readily available in the Annual Report and Accounts. Although 'Chairman's Statements' need always to be taken with a pinch of salt, there may well be some comments you can use as ammunition. Ensure that your information is up to date and accurate - don't base your argument on hearsay. What are the future plans for the company? If they are expanding and having to invest large sums on capital equipment then there may be a little left over with which to augment staff salaries. Is there a long list of creditors - more than the previous year? Perhaps the best time to re-negotiate is during a period of consolidation after expansion, and soon after publication of the annual accounts.

It's quite possible, of course, that when they say that they can't afford it then they mean it. If your company is going through a tough time then you may simply have to put the re-negotiation on hold. The obvious way of cutting back on costs is to shed staff and/or cut pay, and if they perceive *you* to be the 'Trojan horse' your job could be one of the first to go. Keep a keen eye open for the tell tale signs of impending redundancies, e.g. managers becoming unusually friendly, after hours meetings of senior staff and panic measures such as cutting back on the use of equipment and ancillary 'perks'.

'It would set a precedent'

Their objection may not be based primarily on the idea of giving you more. In principle they may be with you all the way. They may fear that an exception made for you would precipitate an unseemly rush by others expecting the same. Setting a precedent is such a fear in some companies it's a wonder anything gets done at all. But this objection can be overcome if you can build a solid argument to suggest that *you really are* a special case. What your employer needs is for you to provide a sound rationale that cannot be applied to anyone else.

'Who are you?'

It's often the case that you can only negotiate a higher salary by linking it to some form of promotion or simply taking on additional responsibilities. Any success here, then, must depend on your ability to assure them that *you have what it takes.* Much will depend upon the type and size of the organization you are in, but it's quite possible that the party with the power to offer you a better deal will have no idea who you really are. You may, for example, be talking with an HR specialist who is very dependant on information received by a third party, e.g. your line manager. The success of your re-negotiation will then hinge on the quality of this information. It might be a big mistake for you to rely totally on this. The danger in so doing can be even greater if there's a communication barrier, or you just don't get on with that third party. And we already know that people come and go - a change of boss immediately prior to your planned re-negotiation can set you back a whole year. It would be unwise then to rely totally on a third party to present a good case for you.

How hard do you push your claims for promotion or for taking on new responsibilities? There's more to it than just letting people know that you want to progress. Do you indicate that *you have what it takes?* The personal qualities to progress 'in house' are exactly those required to secure a better position outside. You must do a self-marketing job so that you and your talents become *visible* to those who are in a position to influence your future.

You may achieve excellent results in your job but this becomes irrelevant if you keep yourself in the background. It may even encourage them to keep you exactly where you are. Understandably perhaps, some employers are often reluctant to change a winning formulae, and if your immediate superiors are pleased with your work it may be in their personal interests to adopt a 'if it ain't broke don't fix it' stance.

The world of work is full of un-sung heroes who regard 'personal trumpet blowing' as somehow demeaning, which is odd because in the world of business it's called 'sales and marketing' and seen as quite the thing to do. To enhance your position you must be prepared to bang on a few doors - not only must you be able to do the business you must be *seen* to be doing it. Just as excessive humility is the curse of the job hunter it can be a very real barrier to negotiation. Take credit for your achievements and don't allow others to steal your thunder. Identify those people most likely to promote your cause and cultivate them so your relationship grows. Such people need not be senior people in the department you wish to leave; they are more likely to be those in positions of influence in that part of the business you would like to join.

'Not this time'

An outright 'no' to your request may be tempered by an invitation to try again at a later date (like *next* year). It's not unusual for this to be the first line of defense. If you can anticipate that this might happen (perhaps by learning from the experiences of others who have tried it) then this would be a sound argument for putting your request in a year before you actually expect to get a result.

Much will depend on how seriously your employer treats the appraisal - is it a well planned and structured discussion that allows both parties to air their views and set agreed objectives, or is it a two minute chat in the corridor once every two years? If it's the former then refer back to your previous appraisal. Look at what performance and developmental objectives were agreed. Have you achieved or even surpassed them? If not then your case for seeking a pay rise could be severely dented, unless your failure to meet objectives was for reasons outside your control.

Preparing for the appraisal

Look first to see if your company has its own internal policy or set procedure on salary reviews, as you may have to follow that procedure. The annual (sometimes six monthly) performance appraisal may be the best stage for you to act on your desire to re-negotiate or, if the person appraising you is not empowered to negotiate, at least sow the seeds and set up a meeting with the person who is.

Your success will depend on the interest your appraiser has in the meeting and their willingness to seriously engage with it, and with you. You may get a clue to their attitude from the way they describe it. Do they call it a 'discussion', 'meeting' or 'interview'? Should it be the latter then they might see it as a one sided affair, which gives you little opportunity to present any sort of a case and which concentrates largely on any negative aspects of your performance.

The main thing here is that you shouldn't go into any appraisal 'cold'. It makes a great deal of sense to *appraise yourself* beforehand and prepare for the meeting just as you would for a job interview.

Your objective is to prepare a sound argument designed to persuade them to improve on the rewards currently paid. We saw earlier that your negotiating strength decreases if nothing has changed since you originally agreed to take the job on - even when you tell them how well you are doing who could blame them for saying 'well, that's what you're paid for'? So you must identify those things that *have* changed. The concept of 'value for money' is no less important here. If you can show them they are getting better value for money now then this will be in your favor. In effect then, you must be able to show them that the mutually beneficial deal you originally negotiated has now become more beneficial to them than to you.

What factors may have changed? At the meeting it's most likely that the appraiser will be referring to the 'job description'. It should be used as a checklist to ensure that all aspects of your work are discussed, and also an opportunity to make any revisions as may be necessary. The big question for you is 'have I taken on any other responsibilities / tasks that were not part of the original agreement? If so make a list, type it out and have two copies made - you can use this as your part of the agenda at the meeting. Give the other party a copy - it will help them, and you, should they have to present your case further up the line.

Also firmly request that it becomes part of the internal documentation and therefore 'on the record'.

Going back through your job description can be a salutary experience. Typically you'll find that many of the original tasks have long since become outmoded and superseded by others, which carry more responsibility and take more *time.* And yet it was presumably this job description upon which the original salary was based. What were the agreed, if agreed, hours of work? You are selling your time and if you can demonstrate that you are giving additional hours then put a price on it. If you find that the original job description is *really* out of date and bears little relation to what you now do then write out a new one and again type it out and present the appraiser with a copy.

Are you now required to use a skill or skills that were not required when you took the job and for which you were not paid? You must certainly distinguish between those skills that you already possessed and those you have learned while doing the job, as you can hardly expect them to pay you for utilizing a skill that they have trained you in. The responsibilities that might go with that skill may be a different matter. But you may for example have a pre-existing language skill that they have now chosen to take advantage of - at the meeting you should put a price on it.

Are you in the type of job where your performance can be distinguished from those of others in your team and relate it to pay? If so, and if you have not until now been on a performance related salary, perhaps now is the time for you to suggest introducing it. Taking the initiative and asserting yourself in these matters is really up to you. If you can come up with the ideas and present them with clarity and *unemotionally* you may be surprised at what you can achieve.

Conceivably, you could still find that nothing has changed and this gives you no leverage to negotiate. This may be true but don't give up and leave it at that. Can you *make* things change? Maybe you can offer to take on other tasks that neatly dovetail into your role and encourage them to pay you more for doing so. Getting more pay isn't about getting something for nothing, whether negotiating internally or externally. They would certainly be receptive to this idea if you could demonstrate that by 're-shaping the role' the whole operation would be more efficient, cost effective and profitable. Your ideas may even obviate the need for them to hire someone else.

Considering the ultimatum

When considering your request for an increase your employer is bound to weigh up the potential dangers of refusing you. Provided you have made a strong and convincing case and that they can afford to increase your remuneration then they are likely to ask themselves the following questions:

- How important are you to the organization?

- Do you make a direct contribution to the bottom line or is your role a marginal one?

- If you were to leave suddenly do we have human resources/talent to keep things going?

- If you left how long might it take us to recruit a replacement and how much would it cost us?

- If you left would morale be adversely affected and might others follow you?

- Do you have direct contact with customers/clients and how would they feel - might they follow you?

- How would others feel if we increased your salary/package? These are all legitimate questions and they are exactly the same questions that you must ask yourself before entering into negotiations, as the answers will be a good indicator of the true strength of your position. Just as you had to sell your 'uniqueness' in the jobs market you have to sell it again now to have any chance of re-negotiating on pay.

In appraising yourself look at the contribution you have made since joining the organization. If you can quantify that contribution in terms of cost savings or profits then so much the better. Perhaps you can identify ways to make an even greater contribution. If so then sell it.

How does your organization normally recruit people at your level? How did they recruit you? If they were to use an agency to find a replacement for you then this could cost them 33% of your first years salary or more - with no guarantee that the replacement could do the job better than you. Look at the combination of skills that need to be brought to the job. How rare are they in the market place? Remember that the person you are negotiating with may not be aware themselves of what skills you use. If they have a simplistic view of what you do then it's up to you to put them right on that.

Although you need to find answers to all these questions, and some are easier than others, it's not a good idea to voice them at the meeting, and certainly not in the form of an ultimatum. As we've seen earlier, implied or overt threats invariably provoke a response opposite to the one you want. On most occasions then it's enough for all of the above to remain unsaid. The ultimatum should truly be a last resort when all else has failed, i.e. if you have put your case and they have responded negatively and, in your view, unjustifiably. However, never use the ultimatum *if you are not prepared to carry out the threat implicit within it.* If you are not fully prepared to resign and you use it as a bluff, don't be surprised if that bluff is called. Stories are legion of people handing in their resignation, expecting at least a modicum of resistance, only for it to be accepted with indecent haste.

If you *were* fully prepared to take the nuclear option and resign then it would be prudent to activate a job search some two to three months before attempting to re-negotiate. If they refuse your request then you don't want to start cranking up a job search *after* the event. Sometimes, seeing you job hunting is in itself enough to convince them that you mean business. So allowing yourself to be seen to be actively job hunting may be an advantage for you. If they can see that you are on the verge of breaking camp then this might galvanize them into action and shake them out of any complacency they may have had.

You will certainly feel more confident if you can go into a re-negotiation with a written job offer already in your pocket. This *could* be used as a final bargaining chip if all other forms of persuasion have failed. Some employees use this as a form of coercion, i.e. 'I have a better offer - if you can't match it I'm off'. This can work but it has nothing to do with sensible negotiation. After all, if you can give them no additional reasons why they should offer you more money other than the fact that someone else has then your case is not a strong one. Again, no one is indispensable.

Finally, beware of being offered a fancy new job title as an alternative, or part alternative to any increase in pay. Job titles make people feel good, and there's nothing wrong with that. But many grand sounding job titles such as 'director', 'executive', 'vice-president', 'president' and 'consultant' have over the years become de-valued. To some people being the proud holder of the title 'senior sales executive' is worth thousands in prestige value. To more sensible people it's no more than 'an old salesman'.

CONCLUSION

In **Case Study 2** we saw how Michael said that money was not the 'be all and end all'. He was of course right and most sensible people would respond in much the same way. However, we also saw how, in voicing that undeniable truth, Michael encouraged his interviewer to have a perception of him which, *on a business level*, was less than favorable. Achieving job offers and reaching that negotiating table so often requires a compromise between the truth and the wisdom of actually speaking it, and reconciling the two is rarely easy. However, 'How To Negotiate Your Salary' has emphasized throughout that negotiation, if it is to stand any chance of success, takes more than just a 'what you see is what you get' attitude.

There's no doubt that the job search can be a real 'emotional roller coaster' - it can play havoc with our confidence, self esteem, health and, not least, financial well being. Little wonder then that for many this vulnerability destroys any incentive they might have had to negotiate a better deal. It's a sad fact of life that, because of the law of supply and demand and, it must be said, the disposition of some employers to pay as little as they can get away with, not everyone has the leverage, confidence and ability to haggle over the price. 'How To Negotiate Your Salary' has not set out to give you a blueprint but to provoke thought, encourage you to re-assess your attitude towards salary negotiation and give you the confidence to redress the balance. No longer need you acquiesce meekly to aggressive questioning on topics like salary. See yourself as a businessperson and not a 'job beggar'. No one would dispute that money can't buy happiness and health - but it *can* alleviate sorrow and it *can* pay for the operation.

---------◆ ◆ ◆ ---------

Alan Jones has been helping people to find the right jobs for 25 years. He is the author of several books on job search and career building including 'Winning At Interview' and 'Network To Get Work'.

'Winning At Interview' advocates a fresh and radical approach to the whole 'job interview' process and demonstrates that with preparation and the right mental attitude you can win a job offer even when competing with more experienced and better qualified people.

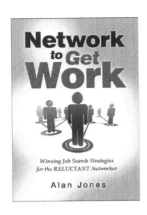

'Network To Get Work' is for those seeking work and needing a clear strategy and sensible guidance on how to apply the principles of networking as an integral part of their job search campaign. If are unsure about networking, and reluctant to involve your contacts in your job search, then this is for you.